PHYSIOLOGY OF CROSS-COUNTRY SKI RACING

PHYSIOLOGY OF CROSS-COUNTRY SKI RACING

by

Ulf Bergh, Dr. Med. Sc.
Department of Physiology
Karolinska Institutet
Stockholm, Sweden

Translated from the Swedish by
Michael Brady and Marianne Hadler

Published under the auspices of
the United States Ski Team

by
Human Kinetics Publishers
Champaign, Illinois

Original title *Langdlopning, Idrottsfysiologi rapport nr. 11*, copyright 1974, Trygg-Hansa Forlagsverksamheten, 10240 Stockholm 5, Sweden.

Published under the auspices of the Sports Medicine Program of the United States Ski Team, as coordinated by Dr. Charles J. Dillman.

Cover photo: Gold medalist Thomas Wassberg of Sweden, just after passing Norwegian Ove Aunli, the Bronze medalist, in the 1980 Winter Olympic Games 15 km race in Lake Placid. Galen Rowell photo.

Library of Congress Catalog Card Number: 81-84643

ISBN: 0-931250-28-5

HUMAN KINETICS PUBLISHERS, INC.
Box 5076
Champaign, IL 61820

Contents

Translators' Preface

Once asked what he would do in a race if his skis were poorly waxed, legendary Swedish racer Sixten Jernberg replied: "Just ski a bit harder."

More than anything else, this taciturn reply embodies the spirit of a country where cross-country skiing is part of the national elan. Although neighboring Norway can perhaps boast more early contributions to the sport of skiing, including the very word "ski," much of what is the present framework of cross-country skiing, particularly racing, in this century is Swedish in origin. Whenever an eager citizens' racer speaks of a "loppet" he/she pays tribute to the first and still largest race of that kind, the annual Vasaloppet, from Salen to Mora in Sweden. Whenever a racer measures aerobic power on an ergometer cycle, he/she not only makes use of procedures developed in Sweden, but also most likely of equipment made there as well.

No small wonder, then, that this book is a Swedish product. But, to place matters in perspective, the original bears the modest title "Idrottsfysiologi, rapport nr. 11, Langdlopning"—"Athletic physiology, report no. 11, Cross-country ski racing." It's simply number 11 in a series on sports, published as a public service by Trygg Hansa, one of Sweden's major insurance companies. As such, it is not a scientific document, but rather a monograph, aimed to inform the skiing public of the physiological background of a national sport.

Terminology currently in use in North America has been used throughout the translation. One Scandinavian term, *elite athlete*, has been retained, as it has no English equivalent. In Scandinavia, athletics is organized almost completely in clubs, and competition emphasizes the individual, not the team in the English sense of the word. The best individual athletes in a sport, from whose ranks the teams formed to represent the country abroad are chosen, are known as the *elite*, the best in the country.

The translators wish to acknowledge the contributions made by Peter E. Sarr, Exercise Physiology Research, University of Ottawa, in thoroughly and meticulously reviewing the translation.

Michael Brady
Marianne Hadler

Foreword

Cross-country ski racing has been of interest in many work physiology studies, so a considerable amount of data on the sport has been accumulated through the years.

In 1954, at the suggestion of Sigge Bergman*, liaison was initiated between the physiologists of the Department of Physiology of the Swedish College of Physical Education, represented by Professor Per-Olaf Astrand, and cross-country ski racers and coaches of the Swedish Ski Federation. The author became involved in this work in 1971, and since has conducted studies of cross-country ski racing training and competition.

In 1971-73, athletic instructor education at GIH (Gymnastik–och–Idrottshogskolan, the Swedish College of Physical Education) included a major subject in cross-country ski racing, which led to systematic study of the sport. The students involved were Jan Hallin, Lena Jansson, Lennart Larsson, Magnus Lindahl, and Bengt Stattin.

The physiology of prolonged, heavy work has often been studied at the Department of Physiology of GIH. These studies have resulted in valuable data, applicable to cross-country ski racing.

This report comprises a summary and discussion of the data gathered and processed from the studies made.

---

*Then director of the Swedish Ski Federation; also former member, now honorary member, of the FIS (International Ski Federation) Council.

Introduction

One goal of this monograph is to analyze the demands that cross-country ski racing places on athletes, through evaluation of those factors which may be decisive for racing performance at various race distances.

Moreover, the purpose has been to examine how elite racers have trained for the past few years, and thereby compare the requirements of training to those of competition.

The explanations of different methods of training are not aimed at a formulation of detailed, general training programs. The intent is rather to provide coaches and athletes with certain basic facts, to aid the planning of training. For this reason, the report begins with a relatively thorough overview of the physiological background.

Much of the research has been contingent upon the cooperation and interest of the Swedish Ski Federation, leaders and athletes. Some of the studies have involved certain uncomfortable tests on the subjects, but nonetheless, they always arrived and did their best.

The author is indebted to Professor Per-Olaf Astrand for valuable suggestions concerning the conduct of the research and the writing of this report.

Physiological Background

Physical performance ability is decided primarily by the following factors:

Energy-yielding processes   aerobic (oxidation)
            anaerobic (fermentation)

Nerve-muscle function   strength
            technique

Psychological factors   motivation
            tactics

Different physical activities combine these factors in various ways. In athletics this means that performance in certain sports depends mostly on the ability to deliver a great amount of energy, while in other sports, performance depends more on the neuromuscular function. Many sports make great demands on all of the factors. Among the sports where performance ability depends strongly on the aerobic energy-yielding processes (with oxygen) are cross-country skiing, long distance running, cycling, rowing, and orienteering. In sprinting, however, the anaerobic energy-yielding processes (without oxygen) are decisive. Examples of sports that place great demands on the neuromuscular function are gymnastics, pole vaulting, and diving. Knowing these various relationships makes it possible to completely or partly estimate the demands made on the athletes in different sports.

By determining, for instance, oxygen uptake, oxygen debt, blood lactate concentration, etc. in top athletes in the sport in question, it is possible to determine the demands of the sport in various situations. Hence, a *work requirement profile* may be made for each sport. The exactness of this profile is decided by many factors, including the accuracy of the available measurements and the possibility of applying them during a competition. By measuring the equivalent parameters of an individual athlete, a *capacity profile* can be determined. In this way, it is possible to compare the demands of the sport and the capacity of the athlete. If, for instance, top athletes within a particular sport, with no exception, have a very high maximum oxygen uptake in proportion to body weight, this is obviously a requirement for improvement. Such studies may then reveal the weaknesses of a particular athlete and serve as a basis for the planning of training.

Energy-Liberating Processes

Energy is needed by many processes which continuously are active in body cells. The metabolism in muscle cells may increase to 100 times its rest value, which is requisite to producing the power needed by a cross-country ski racer. Such power production requires that the muscle cells be supplied with oxygen and energy–yielding substances.

The two primary energy-liberation processes are the aerobic and the anaerobic. In the *aerobic* process, fat, carbohydrates, and proteins are oxidized to liberate energy, and water and carbon dioxide are the by-products:

$$\left.\begin{array}{l} \text{fat} \\ \text{carbohydrates} \\ \text{proteins} \end{array}\right\} + \text{oxygen} = \text{carbon dioxide} + \text{water} + \text{ENERGY}$$

Therefore, oxygen must be available for the process to function.

The *anaerobic* processes function without oxygen. Energy–yielding substances are broken down into those containing less energy, and energy is liberated. The anaerobic energy-yielding processes are:

1) adenosine triphosphate (ATP) = adenosine diphosphate + free phosphate + ENERGY
2) creatine phosphate = creatine + free phosphate + ENERGY
3) glycogen = pyruvate + water + ENERGY = lactate

These energy-yielding substances are stored in muscles, and are therefore immediately available. The quantity of energy so stored is relatively small: Acting alone, energy can be delivered anaerobically for no more than one minute. The final product in the breakdown of glycogen is lactate, a substance which inhibits or impairs muscular work.

Heavy muscular work can be performed for periods of more than one minute only if oxygen is available to the muscles.

Oxygen Transport

The oxygen-transporting organs are lungs, heart, blood, and the circulatory system. Their function is to transport oxygen from the surrounding air to the various body tissues. The transport of oxygen from the inhaled air to the muscle cells thus depends on a range of functions, of which one or several may restrict the transport of sufficient volumes of oxygen.

Lung Capacity

At rest lung ventilation (amount of expired air per minute) is about 5-6 liter/min. At maximum work it is 100-200 liter/min. for well-trained athletes. The increase is due to an increase in respiration frequency (from about 8-10 to 50-60 respirations/min.) and in respiration volume (from about 0.5 liter to about 3-3.5 liter). Lung ventilation may increase further. Therefore, lung ventilation hardly limits maximum oxygen uptake, except perhaps in work at high altitudes (1200 m above sea level or higher).

Later the oxygen reaches the alveoli and there diffuses through the thin walls of the small blood vessels (the lung capillaries) to the blood, where the oxygen is bonded to hemoglobin, as shown schematically in *Fig. 1*. Normally, the transport from the alveoli to the blood is not considered to limit maximum oxygen uptake.

Heart Capacity

The blood, saturated by oxygen in the lungs, returns to the heart, which is the next link in the transport chain. At rest, the cardiac output* is about 5 liter/min. For top athletes in maximum work this capacity may amount to about 40 liter/min. Cardiac output (CO) is determined by heart rate (HR) and stroke volume (SV). This gives:

$$CO = HR \times SV$$

Maximum stroke volume is 100-200 milliliters. The maximum heart rate varies considerably from one individual to another. The average for 25-year-old persons is 195 beats/min. The maximum heart rate decreases (from 10 years of age) with increasing age. On the average it is about 220 - age (in years); for instance maximum heart rate for 50 year olds is on the average of 220 - 50 = 170 beats/min. *(Fig. 2).*

---

*The amount of blood pumped from one chamber per minute.

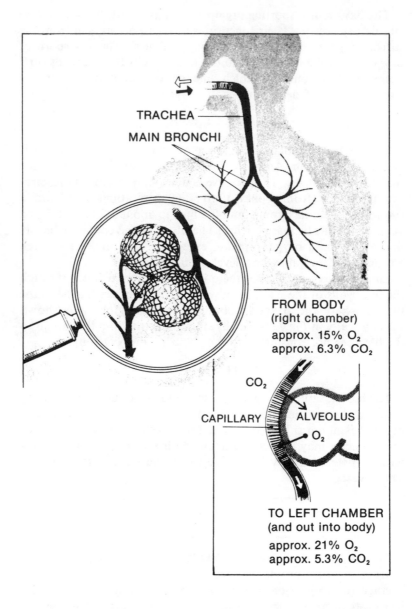

Figure 1. The supply of oxygen to the alveolar ducts and the release of carbon dioxide is due to lung ventilation. In the blood, which returns from the body tissues to the right chamber and is afterwards pumped to the lungs, the oxygen percentage is lower and the carbon dioxide percentage is higher than in the alveoli. This is why oxygen diffuses from the alveoli to the blood and carbon dioxide in the opposite direction.

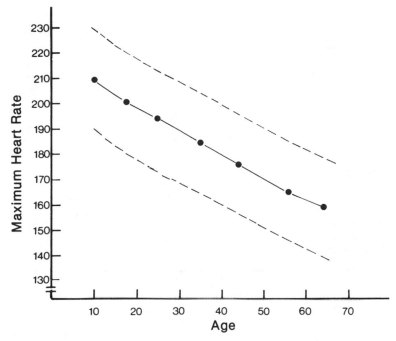

Figure 2. Maximal heart rate for persons of various ages. The solid line indicates the average. Between the dashed lines are the values for 95 out of 100 persons. (After Astrand.)

There are, however, 50 year olds whose maximum heart rate is 195 or more. At rest, the heart rate is normally 50-70 beats/min. The resting heart rate of top endurance athletes may be from 35 to 45 beats/min.

The increase in cardiac output in the transition from rest to work is made by an increase—both in stroke volume and heart rate. When the oxygen uptake is about 40-50% (HR = 110-115) of maximum, the stroke volume will not increase any more and all increases in cardiac output are through increases in the heart rate. Training increases the maximum oxygen uptake. The major part of this increase is due to an increase in cardiac output, which in return is due to an increase in stroke volume. *Table 1* sums up the effect of two months of training by men 20 to 25 years old and gives the estimates for top endurance athletes.

The high maximum oxygen uptake of top athletes is made possible by a higher cardiac output, which is due to a higher stroke volume. Top athletes also have greater heart volumes, blood volumes, more blood vessels, and increased total hemoglobin. However, the hemoglobin concentration does not seem to increase through training; it rather tends to decrease.

Table 1. Representative data received partly from relatively inactive 20-25 year olds before and after two to four months of extremely intense training and partly from a group of top athletes in endurance sports (from Saltin).

| | Two months' training | | Elite endurance athletes |
	Before	After	
Oxygen uptake 1/min	3.1	3.6	5.6
Oxygen uptake ml/kg × min	42	49	75
Arterio-venous diff, vol-percent	14.4	15.5	15.6
Cardiac output 1/min	21.5	23.2	36.0
Heart rate, beats/min	196	192	190
Stroke volume	110	122	189
Heart volume	740	820	1140
Blood volume	4.3	4.6	

Oxygen-Transport Capacity of Blood

One liter of blood in males contains normally 150 gr hemoglobin (Hb), and in females about 130 gr. One gr hemoglobin can bond 1.34 milliliter oxygen. Accordingly, one liter blood in males can bond about 200 milliliters of oxygen (0.2 liter).

The blood which returns from the lungs to the left ventricle, and which is afterwards pumped to the aorta, is usually almost completely saturated with oxygen; that is, almost all the hemoglobin is bonded to oxygen. (During maximum work the oxygen saturation decreases towards 90%, but this is compensated by a concentration of the blood. Thus the oxygen volume in each liter of blood remains constant or even increases.) The blood is pumped from the heart to the muscle and other tissues where some of the oxygen is consumed. The blood then returns to the right ventricle, from where it is afterwards pumped to the lungs, where it is again saturated with oxygen, and at the same time releases carbon dioxide. Out of the 200 milliliter oxygen/liter blood that leaves the heart, about 150 milliliter/liter will, at rest, return through the veins to the heart; 50 milliliter/liter has thus been consumed. The difference between oxygen volume in arterial blood and oxygen volume in mixed venous blood is called arterio-venous oxygen difference (a-v O_2 difference). This can, at maximum work, be about 170 milliliter/liter blood. It is important that the oxygen–rich blood from the heart is fed to the needy muscles. Table 1 indicates that training may increase the arterio-venous oxygen difference slightly; a higher amount of the available oxygen is consumed. Even after many years of training, this increase is relatively small. The increase also is limited; partly because it is impossible for all the blood to go to the tissues which have a high oxygen consumption and partly because the oxygen-bonding ability of the blood is restricted by the hemoglobin percentage (number of red blood cells). Theoretically, an increase in the hemoglobin percentage should result in an increase in the oxygen-bonding ability. It has also been proved by experiments that a marked increase in the Hb percentage in certain cases may improve performance ability. However, an increase in the Hb percentage of the blood increases the viscosity of the blood (blood flows slower), which places an extra burden on the circulatory system. Men have a higher Hb percentage than women, which seems to have a positive influence on maximum oxygen uptake. There is, however, probably an optimal value for the Hb percentage of the blood.

Oxygen-Uptake Ability of Muscle Cells

The oxygen which is transported from the heart is of no value for muscle work if it is not used by the muscle cells. Thus the oxygen uptake at maximum armwork is considerably less than at maximum legwork, in spite of equal heart pumping power in both cases. The explanation is, among others, that the total muscle mass, engaged in armwork, is not large enough to exploit the oxygen-transporting organs maximally. Those who have done extensive arm training, such as canoeists, may on the other hand utilize up to 90% of maximum oxygen uptake in working with their arms. In these persons the muscle mass engaged in work is relatively larger than in persons not specifically arm-trained. Besides, muscle cells may adapt and, according to recent research, increase their oxidation capacity.

At rest, oxygen uptake is 0.2-0.3 liter/min. In many work forms, it increases linearly with the intensity of the work (watt, running speed, etc.) up to a point where it ceases to increase though the intensity of the work continues to increase *(Fig. 3)*. This level is called *maximum oxygen-uptake ability* or maximum *aerobic power*. It varies from one person to another, and may be from 2 to 7.5 liter/min. dependent on inherited characteristics, age, sex, body size, and training conditions.

The connection between the different parts of oxygen transport (lung ventilation excluded) can be expressed as:

Oxygen uptake = HR x SV x a-vO$_2$ difference

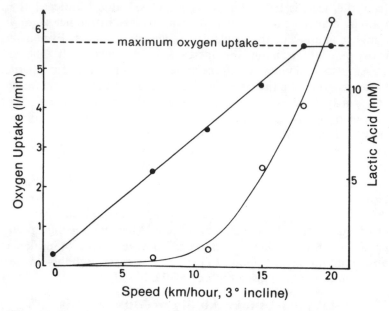

Figure 3. Steady-state oxygen uptake and blood lactate concentration as functions of work intensity on an inclined treadmill. (After Saltin.)

Elite distance athletes differ from average individuals in that they have far greater stroke volumes and therefore greater cardiac outputs and slightly greater a-vO$_2$ differences.

Energy Sources

Food supplies the body with energy in the form of fats, carbohydrates, and proteins. Protein has normally no importance as fuel for muscle work. It functions primarily as a material in production of new cells. Thus fat and carbohydrates serve as fuel for muscle work. The proportions of fat consumption versus carbohydrate consumption are decided by the food composition and the intensity of the work duration, and kind of work (for instance, arm or leg work). The share of carbohydrate consumption increases with the intensity of work (from 70% of maximum oxygen uptake and more).

Fat and carbohydrates may be stored in the body. Carbohydrates are stored as glycogen in the muscles (300-500 gram) and in the liver (40-50 gram). Fat is stored subcutaneously and in the abdominal cavity. The fat "reservoir" of "normal weight" 20-25 year old males amounts to about 10% of body weight, and for females of the same age, about 20% of body weight (corresponding North American figures: 15% for males, 24% for females).

Carbohydrates enter energy liberation when glycogen is broken down to glucose which, in turn, is broken down to pyruvic acid *(Fig. 4)*. The energy liberated in this process is relatively small. The major part of the energy is delivered when the pyruvic acid is "burned," forming carbon dioxide and water. This "burning" requires oxygen. If the oxygen supply to the muscles is inadequate, the pyruvic acid is transformed to lactic acid, which inhibits muscular work capacity.

The process of using fat as a fuel starts with a breakdown of fat

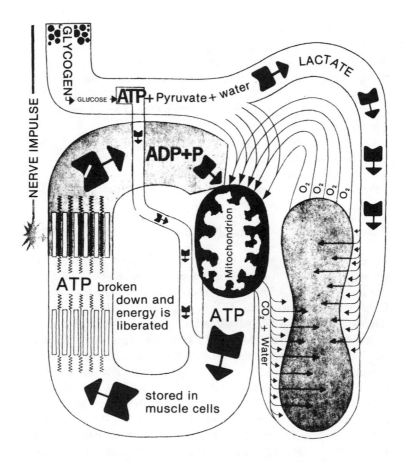

Figure 4. Schematic description of the breakdown of glycogen in muscles and the production of adenosine triphosphate (ATP). The figure indicates the state of heavy muscle work with insufficient oxygen transport; see text. (If sugar glucose is absorbed from the blood, it is connected to the circuit with "glycose"—that is, glycose-6-phosphate—and if fat-free fatty acids are absorbed from the blood, they would be connected to the circuit instead of pyruvate. This is, however, unlikely in the case described here but occurs, for instance, in prolonged work.) (After Karlsson et al.)

in the body reservoirs to glycerol and free fatty acids, which are transported by the blood to muscle cells, where it is oxidized, releasing energy and water and carbon dioxide as by-products. For prolonged heavy work, such as cross-country ski racing, glycogen utilization is responsible for the major portion of the energy liberated. As the body's glycogen stores are limited, carbohydrate deficit may occur if the work period exceeds 1.5 to 2 hours.

Transformation of Chemical Energy Into Mechanical Energy (Muscular Work)

The energy liberated by oxidation of fat and carbohydrates does not result directly in muscle contractions. The only energy source which can directly yield energy for muscle contraction is ATP (Adenosine triphosphate). When nerve impulses stimulate muscles to contraction, ATP is broken down to ADP (Adenosine diphosphate) plus free phosphate and energy. This energy is directly applied for muscle work.

Normally, there is a small ATP reservoir in the muscle, which can be used initially in work, but thereafter ATP continually must be replaced. The oxidation of carbohydrates and fat yields energy in the form of ATP, which again can be used for muscle contraction.

Interplay Between Aerobic and Anaerobic Processes

The energy-yielding processes are described on page 2. Usually, the energy required for most activities is supplied both aerobically and anaerobically. The final stage of the transformation of chemical energy into work, ATP = ADP + P + Energy, is always anaerobic, while ATP subsequently may be replenished both anaerobically and aerobically. At rest, all required ATP is produced by aerobic processes. When heavy work starts, the oxygen transport system initially cannot supply adequate oxygen to the muscles to produce the required amount of ATP. But after a few minutes at this work level, respiration and circulation have adapted so the supply of oxygen is adequate and ATP is replenished aerobically *(Fig. 5)*. In the interim, before the adjustment is complete, the energy required in the muscles must be produced anaerobically. The amount of energy stored in the form of ATP and creatine phosphate is small; therefore, the breakdown of glycogen supplies most of the initial energy metabolism at the beginning of the work.

For instance, in a 1500 meter race at high competition speed, the energy demand is so high that it cannot possibly be met by aerobic processes alone. The anaerobic processes then supply energy, not

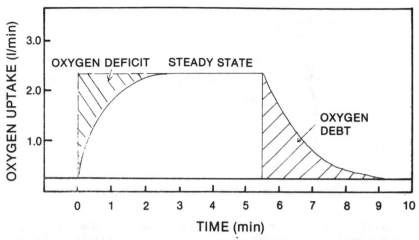

Figure 5. Oxygen uptake at rest during and after light or medium muscle work. (After Astrand.)

only in the first few minutes of activity, but during the entire activity period *(Fig. 6)*. Sometimes the oxygen used in the tissues exceeds the actual oxygen uptake: an *oxygen deficit* occurs. Oxygen deficit may occur in cases other than that mentioned above whenever, during an activity, there is a sudden increase in intensity, such as a sprint.

The lactate formed diffuses to the blood and is transported to the liver, other resting muscles, and the heart, where it is oxidized or synthesized to glycogen (up to 80-85% is synthesized to glycogen, while about 15-20% is oxidized). Synthesis requires energy, which is supplied by oxidation. The result is that after cessation of activity, the oxygen uptake exceeds the normal rest level (Figs. 5,6). The extra oxygen uptake is termed *oxygen debt*, and in addition to the functions discussed above, it builds up ATP and creatine phosphate reservoirs and the oxygen reservoirs in the muscles and the blood.

Generally, increases in oxygen deficit produce still greater increases in oxygen debt, by a factor of 2 or 3. One reason is that glycogen synthesis from lactate requires more energy than that obtained by the breakdown of glycogen. The underlying physiological reasons are not well understood.

Muscles contain a substance known as myoglobin, which is related to blood hemoglobin, and can carry oxygen and less carbon monoxide than does hemoglobin. At rest there is a total of about 0.5 liter oxygen bonded to the myoglobin. If oxygen demand during work is 5 liter/min., these reservoirs can be exhausted in 6 seconds. If the work is characterized by very short (10-15 sec.), in-

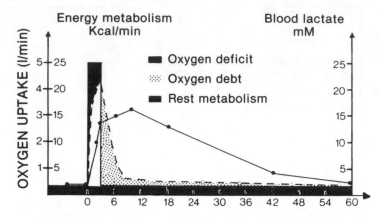

Figure 6. Work which can be performed for a maximum of 3 min. The total energy metabolism during the work is 25 kcal/min (1 = 75 kcal for the total work), only a portion of which is covered by oxygen which is transported to or stored in the muscle groups involved. The oxygen uptake (circles) accelerates but does not reach maximum until the final stage of the work. To meet the additional energy demand, anaerobic processes function so lactate accumulates in the working muscles and diffuses gradually into the blood and is finally carried away. The lactate concentration in the blood reaches its highest value about ten min after the beginning of the work. The shaded area indicates the total oxygen debt. (Data from B. Diamant, J. Karlsson, and B. Saltin.)

tense work periods alternating with rest or light work, these oxygen reservoirs are very important, as they can cover the major part of the oxygen demand during the work periods (see pages 57-58).

The Oxidation of Fats Versus Carbohydrates

As discussed previously, the share of the carbohydrate oxidation in the total energy metabolism increases with increasing work intensity. This change in the choice of fuel is adapted to its purpose, as carbohydrates require less oxygen than fat to produce a given amount of energy. The oxidation of fat alone yields 4.7 kcal (19.7 kilojoule) per liter consumed oxygen. The corresponding value for carbohydrates is 5.05 kcal (21.2 kilojoule). In extremely heavy muscle work, for instance a 10 km ski race, when the possibilities to supply muscles with oxygen are almost totally exploited, it is profitable to use the fuel which yields the most energy per liter consumed oxygen.

Fat has other disadvantages as a fuel for heavy muscle work; it must be broken down to free fatty acids and be transported by the blood to the muscles, and these breaking processes are slower than those for glycose. Moreover, fat cannot be used if oxygen is not available.

In prolonged work the situation is somewhat different. If the work is of intensity that requires no more than 60-70% of maximum oxygen uptake, fat oxidation assumes an increasing part of the energy metabolism as the work goes on. If, on the other hand, the load on the oxygen-transporting organs is more than 75% of maximum, carbohydrate burning will be consistently high until the glycogen in the working muscles is consumed. Then the individual is forced either to stop working or to slow down considerably.

Neuromuscular Function

Properties of Muscle

Muscles are built up of bundles comprising thousands of long, thin muscle cells (muscle fibers), which contain the contractile elements, the myofibrils *(Fig. 7)*. Around the muscles, muscle bundles, and muscle fibers is a thin layer of binding tissue. Muscle fibers have various mechanical and physiological properties. There are two main types of muscle fibers, "red" and "white." The red or tonic fibers are characterized by a large number of mitochondria; the capillaries are tightly packed in the fibers, and the fibers have high oxidizing capacity. The white or phasic fibers, on the other hand, have fewer mitochondria. White fibers can produce more force than red fibers and also reach their maximum tension considerably faster than do red fibers. This is why the white fibers are called *fast twitch fibers* and the red fibers are called *slow twitch fibers*.

The functional units of muscles consist of a number of muscle fibers which contact the same nerve cell. The nerve cell, together with the muscle fibers it innervates, is called a motor unit. When the nerve cell conducts impulses to the muscle fibers, all the fibers in the motor unit are contracted. The more motor units involved, the more force can be produced by the muscle. Because the red fibers produce little force, these are stimulated when the force demand is low, while the white fibers are stimulated when greater muscle force is required. The muscle force may also vary through a change in the contraction frequency of the various motor units.

In relatively light work, such as walking, the slow fibers thus are connected. When greater force is required, such as in a 100 meter race, primarily white fibers are engaged.

The threshold value between the stimulation of nerve cells and the conduction of stimuli to the muscles differs for different cells and obviously is highest for the cells of the fast fibers.

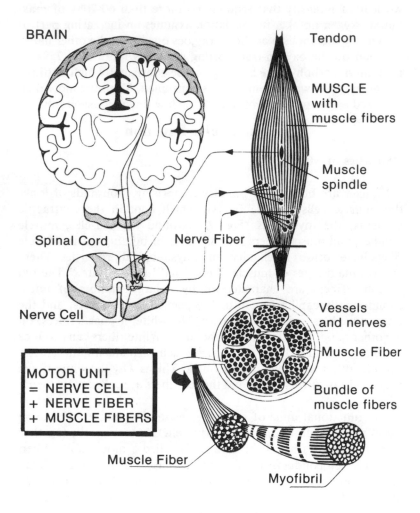

Figure 7. Schematic description of the neuromuscular function. Impulses from the cerebral cortex are conducted via nerve fibers in the spinal cord. In the spinal cord are the nerve cells, in which the impulses are switched to be transmitted to the muscle fibers. Such a nerve cell, together with the nerve fiber and the muscle fibers it innervates, is called a motor unit. In the muscles we find muscle spindles which regulate the muscle tension in various states. The individual muscle fibers in the skeletal muscles are built up from the different substances so that under a microscope they are seen to have a striated or banded structure. These fibrils are responsible for muscle contraction.

Muscle Strength

In principle, muscles work in two different ways: dynamically and statically (isometrically). By dynamic work it is meant that the muscle works by lengthening or shortening. Static work implies that the muscle works without any change in its length. During static work, the muscle is continuously contracted and the pressure in the muscle may be so high so as to restrict or stop blood flow completely. The muscle cells are then forced to work anaerobically and lactate is produced. The lactate cannot be removed as the blood flow in the muscle is weak or has ceased. Therefore, static work is most often experienced as very tiring.

In dynamic work, muscles alternate, contract, and relax, so blood passes regularly through the muscle.

Both dynamic and static work can have maximal as well as endurance characteristics.

The effect of strength training is extremely specific; that is, the effect is related to the exact movement and the type of strength which is trained. If dynamic endurance is trained, it normally improves considerably, while the other types of strength are mostly unaffected.

Technique (Coordination)

A perfect coordinated movement assumes that the right muscle, at the right instant, contracts by the right force, at the same time that other muscles are prevented from working. This places great demands on the nervous system, particularly as it is often a question of adapting the movement to an innumerable variety of external circumstances. In the exercising of a completely new movement these requirements cannot be fulfilled by the interplay of nerves and muscles, and often the precision will be poor and the speed slow, while the overall performance seems stiff and clumsy. One reason is that other muscles than those that are most appropriate for the movement take part in the movement. In many cases even muscles which obstruct the movement are active.

If a movement is repeated sufficiently often, the neural pathways most appropriate for the movement will exhibit some accomodation, while the impulses in other pathways are obstructed. Important also is the fact that a muscle in its work and its capability of producing force is partially directed by sensory cells in the muscles (muscle spindles) and tendons (tendon organs). These sensory cells, like the nerve cells in the brain, can sometimes inhibit, sometimes promote the interplay between nerves and muscles. This helps to explain why many athletes have experienced performance changes from day to day, though motor power is the same.

Measurements

Oxidation Process (Aerobic Process)

The magnitude of the oxidation processes can be determined by measuring the body's capacity to consume or take up oxygen. This is done by having a subject work maximally on a cycle or treadmill for three to eight minutes while air exhaled is collected in a Douglas-bag. The air volume is determined and the air is analyzed for oxygen and carbon dioxide content. The oxygen uptake is given by the relationship:

Oxygen uptake = oxygen in inhaled air − oxygen in exhaled air.

Inhaled air always contains 20.94% oxygen, so the relationship may be stated:

$$\text{Oxygen uptake} = \text{Ventilation} \times \left(\frac{20.94}{100} - \frac{\text{percent oxygen in exhaled air}}{100} \right)$$

The method is accurate to ± 3% in measurements of maximum oxygen uptake, and to ± 1.5% in measurements of submaximum oxygen uptake. All oxygen uptake figures stated in this report have been measured with this method. The method has the drawback that it is somewhat cumbersome to administer: It cannot, for example, be used to measure oxygen uptake during an actual ski race. In such cases, the relationship between pulse and oxygen uptake may be used *(Fig. 8)*.

By measuring the heart rate in racing, the oxygen uptake and thus the oxidation process' share in the energy supply can be determined. In racing, the heart rate may be affected by more than the circulatory demand, such as by nervous tension. However, in the extremely heavy work involved in skiing, there is not much "room" for a nervous heart rate increase. In order to estimate in which degree psychological factors affect the heart rate during a race, the oxygen uptake and the heart rate can be measured later, when the subject runs the same distance at the same speed as in the race in question.

A telemetry system is used to measure the heart rate during a ski race *(Photo 2)*. The racer has a small radio transmitter fixed to his body. Through electrodes the electrical activity in the heart is conducted to the transmitter, which transmits the signals to a receiver connected to a ECG recorder. The range of the transmitters normally used may vary from 50 meters to 2000 meters.

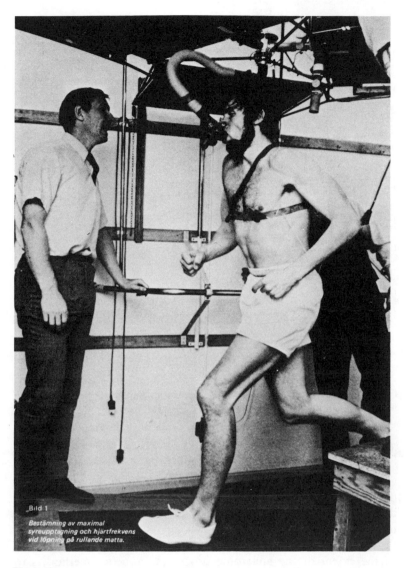

Photo 1
Measuring maximum oxygen uptake and heart rate while subject runs on a treadmill.

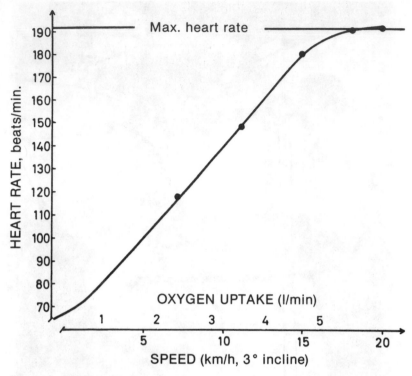

Figure 8. Relationship between heart rate and oxygen uptake. Note the large linear range. (After Karlsson et al.)

The Breakdown Processes (Anaerobic Processes)

Direct measurement of the magnitude of anaerobic processes is difficult, as no exact quantifying methods are available. Oxygen debt traditionally has been measured indirectly by Douglas-bag methods, through gathering exhaled air for at least an hour after the finish of a race. But this method provides only a rough measure of the extent of the anaerobic processes. A better method is to measure oxygen deficit (see Fig. 6). This requires that oxygen demand at different running speeds be determined, which is difficult for higher speeds where oxygen demand cannot be measured in terms of oxygen uptake directly, and where it is uncertain whether the relationship between oxygen uptake and running speed is linear.

Blood lactate level provides no quantitative information on the magnitude of the anaerobic processes because neither the volume of fluid in which the lactate has diffused nor its concentration in tissues or voids is known. If blood samples are taken after the cessation of work, which is the customary procedure, the lactate

Photo 2
Checking telemetry equipment for heart rate measurements. The subjects are holding the telemetry transmitters in their hands. The receiver is to the right and is connected to the recorder in the middle of the photo.

most likely has already begun synthesizing into glycogen, and oxidizing to carbon dioxide and water. However, blood lactate level yields useful measures for extreme cases, that is, whether the anaerobic contribution has been small or large. More recently, blood lactate level has been measured in working muscles using biopsy techniques, which gives a better index of anaerobic energy transfer.

Determination of Fat and Carbohydrate Oxidation, Muscle Fiber and Their Enzyme Activity

There are two methods of determining which type of "fuel," fat or carbohydrate, is oxidized:

1) Determination of the respiratory quotient (RQ)

$$RQ = \frac{\text{volume of carbon dioxide produced}}{\text{volume of oxygen consumed}}$$

RQ is determined from the analysis of exhaled air. It ranges from 0.71 when only fats are oxidized, to 1.00 when only carbohydrates are oxidized. If fat and carbohydrates oxidize to yield equal amounts of energy, RQ is 0.85. Hence, RQ provides a measure of the proportions of fat and carbohydrates oxidized.

2) Muscle biopsy

Biopsy involves sampling small pieces of muscle tissue, 10-20 mg taken with a 3-4 mm diameter (approximately no. 14) needle, and analyzing the tissue for glycogen content. If performed before, during, and after an activity, the test provides a measure of glycogen consumption in the muscle.

Both of these methods are difficult to use in races, partly because of time. The first method requires that exhaled air be gathered and the second that the racer stop for 30 seconds. With the biopsy technique, one may, however, take samples before and after a race. This requires only local anesthesia in the skin and the test is so uncomplicated that heavy muscle work can be done immediately afterwards.

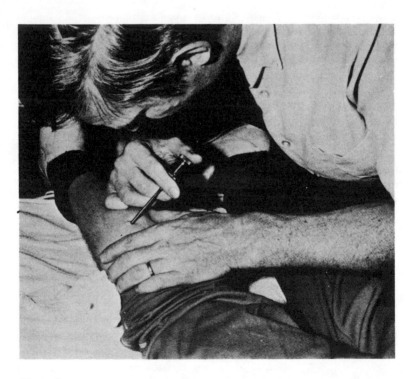

Photo 3
Taking biopsy of muscle from calf.

A biopsy may also be analyzed for ATP and creatine phosphate content, plus activity of the various enzymes. Furthermore, the muscle sample may be cut into thin slices, dyed, and photographed under a microscope, which makes it possible to determine the number of fast and slow fibers and also the number of mitochondria.

Measuring Strength

Cross-country skiing is primarily endurance dynamic muscle work. For this type of strength there are now no measurement methods suitable for application in races. In the laboratory, such measurements can be performed, even if the methods are not as exact as those for determining oxygen uptake.

Evaluating Technique

The muscles activated, their degree and duration of contraction, and the chronological order in which they participate in an activity can be evaluated by *electromyography (EMG)*, which involves measuring and recording motor unit potentials.

Another method of evaluating technique involves measuring energy metabolism (oxygen uptake) for a given exercise, such as running at a set speed. The lower the oxygen uptake for the exercise involved, the better the technique or the greater the efficiency. This method has a drawback in that it may only be applied for work intensities where all energy metabolism corresponds to an oxygen demand which is less than the subject's maximum oxygen uptake; that is, no energy is delivered by anaerobic processes.

Subjects

Subjects have been selected from various groups of individuals, with age ranging from 11 to 70 years. Both male and female athletes of world-class level have been involved.

Results and Discussion

Maximum Oxygen Uptake (Maximum Aerobic Power)

Values of maximum oxygen uptake for Swedish male elite skiers (1963), Swedish male and female elite skiers (1973), present elite skiers (with dates), GIH physical education students, and two world-class runners are given in *Fig. 9*. For elite male ski racers, the values as shown are seldom below 5.5 1/min. or 80 ml/kg × min. World-class distance runners also have values in the range 80-89 ml/kg × min. For female elite ski racers, the values are 3.5 - 4.4 1/min. or 70-75 ml/kg × min. Unfortunately, no values for world-class female distance runners were available when the figure was drawn; in 1970 female Swedish elite runners had a value of 60 ml/kg × min.

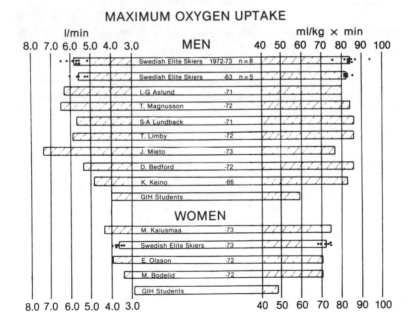

Figure 9. Maximum oxygen uptake for male and female elite cross-country ski racers, world-class runners, and GIH physical education students. Average values are for Swedish male and female elite athletes. Points shown are for individuals.

As can be seen from Fig. 9, world-class cross-country ski racers are characterized by extremely high maximum aerobic power, both total, in 1/min. and in proportion to body weight, in ml/kg × min. This corroborates racing situations, since racing times for men are a minimum of about 30 minutes and for women a minimum of about 16 minutes. In these cases, the aerobic processes account for respectively 95% and 90% of the total energy metabolism (Karlsson et al., 1967).

For longer races, 30 km and 50 km, the corresponding values are at a minimum of 98% (Astrand et al., 1963), that is, the anaerobic contribution is small *(Table 2)*.

During the 1955 Swedish national championships, maximum oxygen uptake was measured on some of the best racers. The results are given in *Table 3*. In this case, the trophy list appears to have been ranked in order of maximum oxygen uptake.

The relation between maximum oxygen uptake and race results for the five best placings for six Swedish national team racers during the winter of 1972 are shown in *Fig. 10*. The data shown imply that results in racing are more related to oxygen uptake in ml/kg × min. than in liter/min. However, there are several known cases of racers who, in spite of a relatively low maximum oxygen uptake per kilogram body weight (see Fig. 9), are among the world elite. Such racers will then have extremely high total oxygen uptake in

Table 2. Aerobic and anaerobic energy liberation at maximum work of duration from 10 seconds to 120 minutes (after Astrand).

Process	Duration of maximum work							
	10 sec	1 min	2 min	4 min	10 min	30 min	60 min	120 min
ANAEROBIC								
kcal	25	40	45	45	35	30	20	15
percent	85	65-70	50	30	10-15	5	2	1
AEROBIC								
kcal	4	20	45	100	250	700	1300	2400
percent	15	30-35	50	70	85-90	95	98	99
Total (kcal)	29	60	90	145	285	730	1300	2400

Table 3. Maximum oxygen uptake (while skiing) and placings in the 1955 Swedish national championship 15 km race (after Astrand).

Subject	Maximum oxygen uptake 1/min	ml/kg × min	Result in 15 km
S.J.	5.88	81.7	1
L.L.	5.49	81.3	2
P.E.L.	5.38	80.3	3
S.G.	5.30	79.1	4
G.S.	5.34	78.5	10

liters/min. The situation in cross-country ski racing differs from that of long distance running, where most world-class runners, as far as we know, have a maximum oxygen uptake lower than 5.4 1/min. but over 83 ml/kg × min. This will be analyzed in a later chapter (page 53).

Recordings of heart rate during 10 km and 20 km races show that the rate is maximum or nearly maximum on all uphills, and no

Photo 4
Measurement of oxygen uptake while skiing.

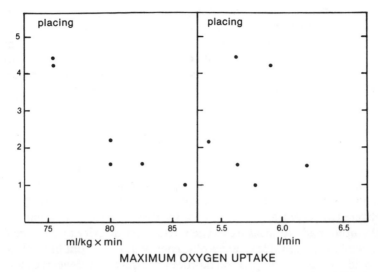

Figure 10. Maximum oxygen uptake and results, averages of five best races of six Swedish national team racers, January-February 1972.

more than 20 beats/minute below maximum on long downhills. For skiing on flats for relatively long periods, two minutes or more, the heart rate was measured at 5 to 15 beats/minute below maximum *(Fig. 11)*. These data certainly depend on course profile, but not to the same extent as is the case for running. The most probable reason is that skiing downhills are covered far faster than in running, so the heart rate does not have time to decrease as much.

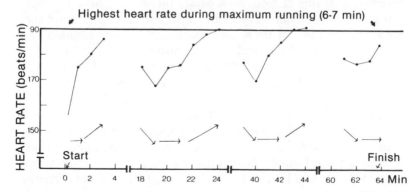

Figure 11. Heart rate of the winner during a 21 km race (3 × 7 km). For technical reasons the rate could not be measured on some parts of the course. Arrows indicate incline: ⟶ = flat, ⟋ = uphill, ⟍ = downhill.

The conclusion is, then, that the demands on the oxygen transport system are exceptionally high, as it is loaded maximally or almost maximally repeatedly during a race, and it seldom operates below 85% of maximum oxygen uptake. A high maximum aerobic power is definitely a requirement for cross-country ski racing but is, of course, no absolute assurance of world-class performance.

Anaerobic Capacity

As previously discussed (Table 2), 90% of energy liberation comes from aerobic processes under maximum work of 15-120 minutes duration. This implies that a portion of the energy is delivered anaerobically, more so for shorter distances. No attempts have been made to measure oxygen debt after activity and thereby evaluate the magnitude of anaerobic energy transfer. But blood lactic acid level after competition has been measured for several cases; the results are given in *Table 4* and *Fig. 12*. Blood lactic acid level decreases with increasing race times. The relationship is nonlinear and applies for race times shorter than three hours. After the shortest races, 5 and 10 km, blood lactic acid is at the same level as after maximum running on a treadmill for five to seven minutes, which implies that the anaerobic contribution is large during portions of the shorter races. This probably applies especially to relays, where tempo is often more uneven than during the individual events. Because samples are taken after races, the results primarily reflect the lactic acid situation during the latter parts of the races. In such situations, anaerobic capacity can certainly be decisive between two otherwise equal racers. Often, no more than a few seconds, or tenths of seconds, separate the top finishers in a race. For a race of 30 minutes duration, 1.8 seconds time difference corresponds to 0.1% in time, and the anaerobic contribution can supply up to 5% of the total energy transfer (see Table 2).

For race distances around 30 km (race times of 85-105 minutes), the anaerobic contribution can be up to a few percent of the total energy transfer. This is confirmed by the relatively high blood lactate, as shown in Fig. 12. Even here, anaerobic capacity can be a decisive indicator. When race times are about three hours or more, blood lactic acid level is low, in spite of maximum sprints. Measurements of muscle lactic acid level after a 55-kilometer race showed that it was low, which indicates that the anaerobic energy transfer was low.

The question is open as to what lies behind this inability to "turn on" the breakdown mechanism.

However, it is possible that lactic acid builds up earlier and then is burned under subsequent phases of a race. This hypothesis is confirmed by the decrease of blood lactic acid level during prolonged, heavy work (Fig. 30). But this cannot explain why blood lactic acid concentration is low, even though the racer sprints maximally.

In summary, it can be said that skiing at an elite level requires very high maximal oxygen uptake (aerobic capacity), and that anaerobic capacity, relatively speaking, plays a minor role, but in

Table 4. Blood lactate level, in mg% and race times for various race distances. (1) Swedish national championships, (2) Tryouts for World Ski Championships. Times are stated in customary decimal notation: 3.06.42 means 3 hours, 6 minutes and 42 seconds.

10km		15km		30km[1]		30km[2]	
Time	Lactate	Time	Lactate	Time	Lactate	Time	Lactate
35.17	139	53.48	94	1.31.50	123	1.50.37	110
35.47	133	53.53	110	1.32.32	91	1.50.41	—
36.09	192	54.56	—	1.32.41	63	1.50.57	69
36.13	144	55.10	100	1.32.47	—	1.51.46	60
36.17	149	55.17	109	1.33.07	94	—	—
36.25	109	55.20	108	1.33.28	118	—	—
36.36	110	55.35	110	1.33.44	—	1.52.58	41
35.57	135	55.39	132	1.33.45	77	1.53.03	52
—	—	55.40	—	1.33.47	—	1.53.03	62

50km		85km	
Time	Lactate	Time	Lactate
3.06.42	39	5.01	—
3.10.30	42	5.06	19
3.10.38	47	6.28	33
3.11.42	59	7.08	22
3.12.12	25	7.50	15
3.14.31	38	8.30	26
3.14.31	31		
3.14.53	—		
3.15.20	—		

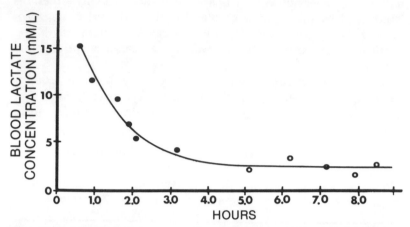

Figure 12. Blood lactate concentration after races of 10 km to 85 km ● median values, 0 individual values. 1 mM corresponds to 9 mg% (After Astrand et al.)

certain cases can be decisive for final results, primarily over shorter distances. This applies of course, only if racers are otherwise equal. Not even an extremely high anaerobic capacity can compensate for low aerobic power.

An important part of the tactical preparation for a race is that the racer learns how high a tempo can be tolerated on uphills such that lactic acid buildup is not so high that recovery is inadequate for the next uphill. Warming up before a race is therefore of great importance, partially such that the race can be started with a relative high oxygen uptake (or lower oxygen debt, and partially such that it is then easier to get a good starting speed.

Oxygen uptake decreases as the altitude of a race increases. If a racer maintains the same tempo at altitude as at lower elevation, lactic acid builds up to a high level (large oxygen debt). In addition, it is more difficult to "get rid of" the lactic acid. The consequence is that one should start more slowly and try to hold as even a tempo as possible. Acclimitization time is desirable, partially to allow the racer to become accustomed to the higher altitude and partially to provide the opportunity to find out how high a tempo can be maintained.

As mentioned above, the time difference between top racers is often less than one percent of the average finish time. Therefore, it is hardly possible to exactly predict result lists on the basis of physiological data, for which measurement inaccuracy is 3% or more. However, racers with similar maximum oxygen uptake often end up near each other on result lists, although not necessarily in consistent order. Other factors, such as technique, endurance, waxing, course profile, "day's form," can determine the ranking of top skiers having approximately the same maximum oxygen uptake (see pages 31-33).

However, it is instructive to compare three Swedish elite skiers *(Table 5)*, who differ in maximum oxygen uptake by 7% and 13%. Race results, expressed as average speed and final result placing, show that measuring maximum oxygen uptake, in this case, gives a very good picture of mutual ranking.

During the Engelbrekts Race in 1969 (55km), maximal oxygen uptake and racing speed at 85% to 90% of maximum oxygen uptake were measured.

For 11 racers, finish times varied from 191 to 296 minutes. The mutual ranking in the finish list is compared with numerical ranks of other variables. The result list ranking agreed very well with the numerical ranking of speed at 85-90% maximal oxygen uptake *(see Table 6)*. However, it should be mentioned that among the subjects in this test, there was a wide range of maximal oxygen uptake, speed for a given oxygen uptake, and finishing time. The percentage of difference between the various persons in finish time and skiing speed at a set percent of maximal oxygen uptake was not very large. This implies that it is more difficult to predict mutual ranking in a result list for a more homogeneous field than this one.

Annual Variation of Maximum Oxygen Uptake

The maximum oxygen uptake capabilities of elite skiers were measured at various times during a year. Usually, but not always, the lowest values were measured in the period from May 15 through June 15, and the highest values at the end of January. Aggregate

Table 5. Maximal oxygen uptake, race speed, and average placing for 3 Swedish elite skiers for races in January and February 1972. (All three raced in the 1972 Olympics and at least three subsequent races.)

Subject	Maximum Oxygen uptake 1/min	ml/kg × min	Average Speed meter/min	Placing
A	5.68	86.1	328	1
B	5.38	80.1	318	6
C	5.89	75.2	314	12

Table 6. Race time and mutual ranking of subjects' physiological variables as well as mutual ranking of finish results (after Wehlin et al.).

Racer	Mutual rank in final results	Maximum Oxygen uptake ml/kg × min	"Technique" Speed at 85%-90% of max. O₂ uptake		Race time minutes
K.E.	1	1	1	(245)	191
B.N.	2	2	2	(213)	206
H.E.	3	5.5	4	(206)	221
B.E.	4	4	3	(208)	229
L.S.	5	3	5	(204)	233
U.Ma.	6	10.5	6	(203)	236
R.L.	7	9	7	(200)	254
A.E.	8	8	8	(195)	255
L.E.	9	7	9.5	(190)	282
U.Mo.	10	10.5	9.5	(190)	290
B.S.	11	5.5	11	(160)	296

differences are 5% to 23%. Different skiers also have considerably differing uptakes. The variation of maximum oxygen uptake for two Swedish elite skiers is shown in *Fig. 13*. Note that the transition from dry-land training to ski training does not affect the maximum oxygen uptake notably for the first two to three weeks, but thereafter, the following five to six weeks training result in an increase of about 5%. The explanation is most likely that the first few weeks skiing is at a relatively easy tempo, 50 to 80 kilometers per day, but thereafter tempo increases and distance often decreases, often being divided up into several tours a day. Time-wise, a major part of training is conducted at high intensity (see page 66). Although compared with dry-land training, the oxygen-transport organs are loaded maximally or almost maximally for longer periods of time (see pages 24 and 66). This is because skiing distributes work load over greater muscle mass than does running on foot, and therefore it is possible to hold a high tempo for longer times, and partially because uphills are closer in time, because skiers are faster on downhills. Some racers at the end of the racing season (end of April) have a relatively small (about 5%) decrease in maximum oxygen-uptake capability, compared with their highest

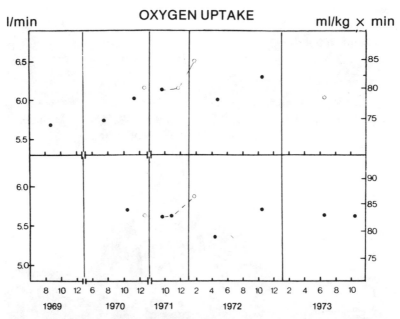

Figure 13. Maximal oxygen uptake at different times of the year for several years in sequence. 0 training on skis; ● dry-land training. Racer T.L. (lower portion of figure) has approximately the same value at the end of dry-land training in 1970, 71, 72 and 73, while racer T.M. (upper portion) increased from 5.68 to 6.30 lit/min. The highest value for both racers was attained in January of each year.

value for the winter. At this writing it is not possible to say whether this decrease starts in January or later. Certainly it is not possible to maintain the same hard training intensity for the entire year, but a decrease of maximum oxygen uptake by as much as 20% is excessive. Variation of 5-10% in May through June is acceptable and necessary, because during the transition from skiing to dry-land training, it is not possible to train hard enough and long enough because of the risk of joint or tendon damage, etc.

However, a competition season should be planned to allow as much training as necessary to retain the January level of oxygen uptake for the time necessary to cover the most important races.

Capability of Prolonged Work

Endurance is defined as the capability to exploit as much as possible of maximum oxygen uptake for longer periods of time (more than 30 minutes).

Aside from maximum oxygen uptake, the capability for prolonged work can be influenced by blood sugar level, muscular glycogen content, liquid balance, etc. In a study of unlike persons,

Galina Kulakova in the 1978 FIS 10 km. Michael Brady photo.

some of whom were very well trained and others very poorly trained, it was found that the capacity for prolonged work is largely determined by the maximum oxygen uptake. However, smaller differences were noted in the ability to work as long as possible at a specified percent of the respective individual's maximum oxygen uptake. The explanation can be that the well trained had higher aerobic powers, whereby they, for instance, at 75% of their maximum oxygen uptake, used more energy. The glycogen stores therefore are depleted equally rapidly for trained as for untrained persons. However, if one compares capabilities of trained and untrained persons, who have the same maximal oxygen-uptake capabilities, the trained person is found to be able to work over a considerably longer period of time. The trained person has a greater capability to stretch out glycogen reserves by burning fats (has a lower RQ; see the chapter on nutrition).

Other studies have shown that when subjects are required to run as fast as possible for 30 minutes the difference between the work intensity of trained and relatively untrained persons is about 5%. Comparison of elite racers and relatively well-trained GIH students (physical education majors at Swedish PE Institute), for running for 90 minutes, have shown the skiers to work at 83% of maximum oxygen uptake and the students at 79%.

The best racers also have a very high maximal oxygen uptake (compare to page 22). The differences named above in endurance are so large that they can be decisive in determining performance. If, for instance, a person with a maximum aerobic power of 80 ml/kg × min. under certain conditions can exploit 80% of his/her maximum oxygen uptake and increase it to 85% after endurance training, the corresponding speed increase is from 18 km/h to 19 km/h *(Fig. 14)*. In a 30 km race, this means a 100 min. finish time, compared to 104 min. If the maximum oxygen uptake is increased by an additional 5%, the average speed increases to 19.85 km/h and the 30 km race time drops to 91 min., assuming that all other factors are constant.

However, extremely high endurance cannot compensate for insufficient, maximal oxygen uptake.

Muscle Fiber Composition and Enzyme Activity

Most endurance athletes have skeletal muscles composed predominantly of slow, often called red, tonic fibers. Studies of Swedish and Finnish elite racers indicate that their arm and leg muscles comprise predominantly slow twitch fibers, respectively 63-91% and 45-100%.

As opposed to runners and cyclists, no elite cross-country ski

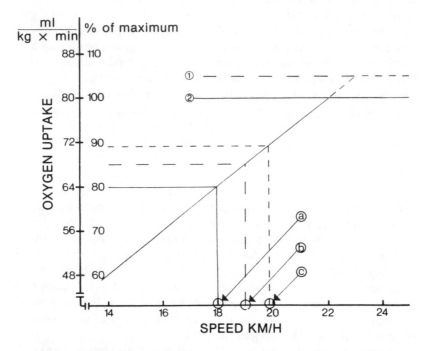

Figure 14. Calculated speed for a person having a maximum aerobic power of 80 ml/kg × min (2)
a) Utilizing 80% of maximum oxygen uptake
b) Utilizing 85% of maximum oxygen uptake
c) Utilizing 85% of maximum oxygen uptake, which is increased by 5% to 84 ml/kg × min (1).

racers (among those tested) have less than 63% slow fibers in their leg muscles. It is not known if this is a result of extensive distance training and/or if the best cross-country ski racers are persons born with predominantly slow muscle fibers. The latter reason seems the most likely.

In cross-country ski racing, with the exception of relays, results are seldom determined by sprints, "man against man," as they are in running and cycling. Therefore, it is unnecessary for cross-country ski racers to have many fast, pale or white, phasic muscle fibers.

For proficient cross-country ski racers, the activity of oxidizing enzymes in muscles of greatest importance in cross–country skiing is approximately double that in the same muscles of untrained persons; in other muscles, the activity is only slightly higher for the trained persons. The activity of those enzymes which function in the breakdown of glycogen seems relatively equal in trained and untrained persons.

Oxidizing enzyme activity in the arm and leg muscles is considerably greater for racers tested in the winter than those tested in May and June *(Fig. 15)*, while the variation in maximum oxygen uptake in most cases is less than 10%.

Other studies indicate that (1) enzyme activity decreases rapidly when training stops, and (2) it takes a long period of training to build up to this level of activity. The situation may also be that maximum oxygen uptake and the activity of the oxidizing enzymes co-variate, and the latter changes to a greater extent *(Fig. 16)*. This is a plausible explanation of the fact that even relatively small differences in maximum oxygen uptake result in large differences in performance ability, both between different racers and for the same individual racer at different times of the year, following changes in endurance. As previously discussed (page 33), elite racers can, for a certain period of time, utilize a greater portion of their maximum oxygen uptake than can well-trained GIH physical education students. The leg muscles of these elite skiers comprise 72-91% slow fibers, while those of the GIH physical education students comprise 63-64% slow fibers. Assuming that each slow fiber has the same activity of oxidizing enzyme activity, which should result in greater endurance. It is also possible that endurance training results in an increased proportion of fat oxidation, which results in the glycogen stores lasting longer.

A study made during the Lindingoloppet (30 km cross-country foot race) showed that those individuals with the greatest percentage of slow muscle fibers as a rule also could maintain the highest average tempo (Fig. 16).

The activity of oxidizing enzymes is greater in trained than untrained persons, even for the fast fibers. The fast fibers of a trained person have approximately the same oxidizing enzyme activity as the slow fibers of untrained persons, which implies that even fast fibers are affected by endurance training, and therefore, are significant in the capability for prolonged work.

How can the fast fibers be engaged in an activity in which they normally do not participate? Apparently, endurance training at an intensity corresponding to 70-90% of maximum oxygen uptake first engages the slow fibers, which subsequently are depleted of their glycogen. Thereafter (1-2 hours), the muscles must engage more fast fibers, which have retained their glycogen stores unchanged. In this manner, even the fast fibers are affected by endurance training.

Overdistance training at submaximum tempo (see above) can therefore contribute to increasing endurance. This should apply

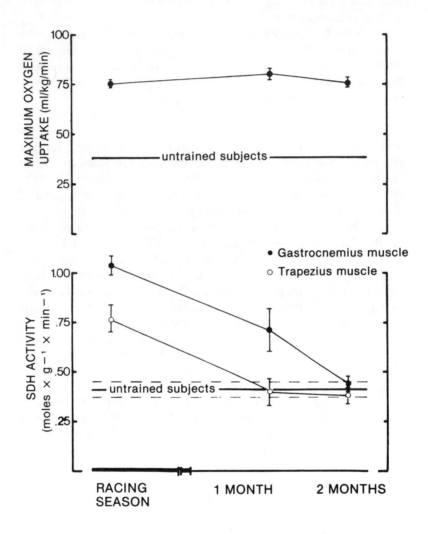

Figure 15. Maximum oxygen uptake and activity of SDH (succinate dehydrogenase, an oxide reductase enzyme) in shoulder and calf muscles of Swedish and Finnish elite racers. Data for untrained persons is also included for comparison. Note that as early as a month after the end of the racing season, the enzyme activity in the shoulder muscles of trained racers is the same as that for untrained persons. (After Karlsson.)

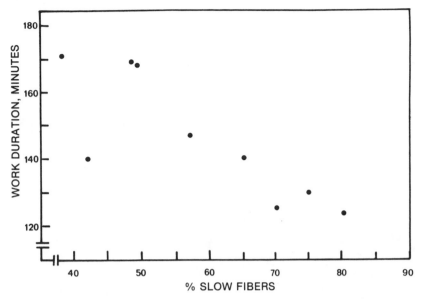

Figure 16. Time for running 30 km vs. percentage of slow muscle fibers in leg muscles. (Costill et al.)

primarily to persons with a relatively large number of fast fibers. On the other hand, persons whose muscles predominantly comprise slow fibers perhaps do not need such extensive quantity of training (2-4 hours per workout). A greater part of their fibers are engaged in the first hour of training. Their training is most likely most effective when divided up into several, shorter workouts. However, several trials are required before any definite rule can be formulated.

The Importance of Diet in Performance Capability

As early as the 1930s, it was found that the food consumed the day before prolonged work can be decisive for performance capability. In these tests, the subject's blood sugar level was found to be very low when work was interrupted, which was probably the reason for feelings of exhaustion. When the subjects consumed glucose (grape sugar), the feeling of exhaustion disappeared and they could continue working for an additional hour. Using biopsy techniques, it is possible to determine how muscle glycogen level changes during work. In one study with 20 subjects (10 trained, 10 untrained), the glycogen level was measured in muscles before the work started and every 20 minutes during work at 75% of the individuals' maximum aerobic power *(Fig. 17)*. After 80-120 minutes work, the subjects were completely exhausted and the glycogen

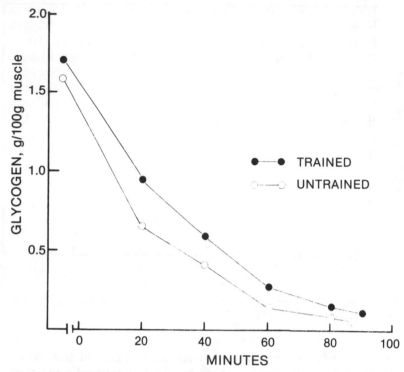

Figure 17. Decrease in muscle glycogen during work at 75% of maximum aerobic power (After Hermanssen.)

level in their muscles was essentially zero. During the entire work period, the RQ constant for the untrained was 0.96 and for the trained 0.91. The computed carbohydrate consumption was virtually constant, approximately 2.7 gram/min., for the entire duration of the work.

During the final 15-20 minutes of the work, when the glycogen level in the muscles was very low, glycogen from the liver was almost certainly used. Exhaustion occurs most likely when the muscle glycogen stores are empty and when blood sugar level is low. These two effects need not necessarily occur simultaneously.

In another study, subjects skied cross-country to exhaustion (119-154 minutes), holding speed constant (corresponding to about 80% of maximum oxygen uptake). RQ was found to be essentially constant during the entire work period, which indicates a constant, high carbohydrate consumption (2.6 g/min).

The glycogen level in muscles at the start of prolonged work can be varied by varying diet the previous day. In one study, subjects consumed different, specified diets and subsequently worked to exhaustion at 75-80% of their maximum oxygen uptake. When they ate a normal, balanced diet, their muscle glycogen level was 1.7%

by weight and the work duration was two hours. For the following three days, the subjects ate fats and proteins. The muscle glycogen level was then 1.0% by weight and exhaustion occurred after a work period of one hour. After three days on a high-carbohydrate diet, the muscle glycogen content rose, in some cases to 4%; work duration was three hours and in some cases, four hours *(Fig. 18)*.

The capability to perform prolonged, heavy muscular work is accordingly strongly dependent on the size of the glycogen stores. The importance of well-filled carbohydrates stores for performance capability in races of 90 minutes duration or more is clearly illustrated by the studies conducted during the 1967 Lidingoloppet (30 km cross-country foot race). The subjects ran the race twice, at an interval of a few weeks, once starting with well-filled glycogen

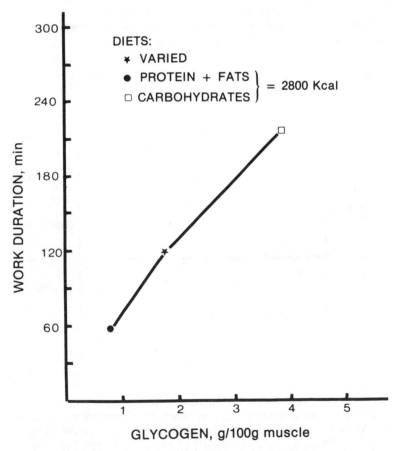

Figure 18. Work duration when subjects cycled to exhaustion with muscle glycogen content varied at start of work. (After Saltin.)

depots and once starting with normally filled stores. Times were taken at several places along the course. The results are shown in *Fig. 19*. From these studies it is apparent that (1) high glycogen content in muscles does not mean that the start tempo can be greater than when starting with normal glycogen content, (2) as glycogen content approaches zero, tempo decreases, and (3) the lower the glycogen content at the start, the earlier the tempo decreases. Muscular glycogen content of 4% or more cannot be achieved only with a high carbohydrate diet, unless the buildup starts with completely empty glycogen depots. The largest glycogen depot (total up to 700 g) can be obtained when muscular glycogen content is held at a very low level for three to four days (through daily training with a diet of protein and fats), followed by a three-day, high-carbohydrate diet, along with rest or low activity level *(Fig. 20)*. Here it should be emphasized that each gram of glycogen surplus results in a weight increase of about one kilogram.

Normally, glycogen stores are about 300-400 grams, which is sufficient for 80-120 minutes of skiing at racing speeds. For race times less than one hour (20 km races), the normal glycogen stores are adequate in all cases. Acute glycogen shortages occur first during

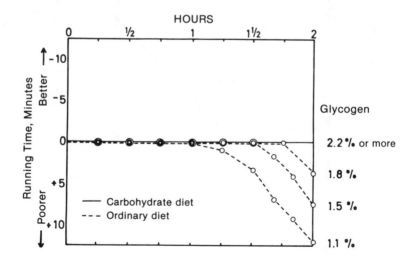

Figure 19. Importance of an adequately high muscle glycogen content when running at high tempo for two hours. The figure shows simplified results from studies made during the Lidingolopet race and during subsequent running on the same course. The solid horizontal line represents intermediate and final times when a high carbohydrate diet preceded the race. The dashed line represents times after consuming an ordinary diet. (After Saltin.)

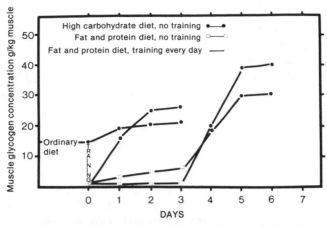

Figure 20. Muscle glycogen concentration with different diets. The highest level results from three days diet of fats and proteins along with hard training every day followed by three days high carbohydrate diet with no training. (After Saltin.)

races of 30 km or more. However, in practice, this happens seldom to elite skiers. The explanation is perhaps that the racers seldom train hard the last three days prior to an important race and on their last day of hard training, essentially empty their glycogen depots. Subsequent consumption of a high-carbohydrate diet and relative rest results in elevated glycogen stores (see Fig. 20).

However, the results of many 50 km races have been decided between 40 km and 50 km. In most cases, losses in these last 10 kilometers can be attributed to emptied glycogen stores and/or low blood sugar.

A low blood sugar level can be increased by consuming sugar during a race. Normally, the blood contains 5-6 grams of sugar. When the level sinks to 3-4 grams, the central nervous system is affected, which relies only on consumption of carbohydrates. The symptoms are fatigue and hunger and, in extreme cases, befuddlement. As the amount of sugar concerned is very small, a few lumps of sugar can do wonders (one lump = 3 grams).

The extent to which muscle cells can absorb sugar from the blood during work is not yet understood. In any case, adequate amounts of glycogen should be stored in the muscles before the race. Sugar consumed during a race can help to maintain blood sugar level and possibly also to support the muscles' requirements for fuel. In all cases, a suitable diet is recommended prior to all longer races. If the racers ski the course the day before the race, they should do so at a low tempo, such that primarily fat is burned and glycogen is saved. It may take up to two days to fill the glycogen stores.

Some Practical Diets For Racing

Race day: Sunday
Race duration:

Less than 80 minutes:	Normal varied diet.
80-100 minutes:	Normal varied diet, with extra carbohydrates on Friday and Saturday.
100-150 minutes:	Thursday morning: Training at least 2-3 hours. Thursday-Saturday: Easy training, high–carbohydrate diet.
150-120 minutes:	Tuesday-Wednesday: Daily training, at least 2-3 hours. High fat and protein diet. Avoid carbohydrates.
	Thursday-Saturday: Easy training or rest. High-carbohydrate diet.
Vasalopp (85 km):	Sunday: Train over corresponding distance, 60 to 90 km.
	Monday-Wednesday: Daily training, at least 2-3 hours. High fat and protein diet. Avoid carbohydrates. Be prepared that training during these three days may be a burden and totally uninteresting.
	Thursday-Saturday: Rest or easy training. High-carbohydrate diet. (Protein and fat can be consumed.)

Examples of:

High-carbohydrate foods	**High-fat foods**	**High-protein foods**
Potatoes	Butter	Lean beef or pork
Root vegetables	Margarine	Mutton or lamb
Fruits and vegetables	Cooking oils	Fish
Bread	Egg yolk	Lean cheese
Butter	Bacon	Liver
Grains	Fat cheeses	Milk
Honey	Hot dogs	
Sugar	Cream	
Rice		
Macaroni		
Beans		
Peas		

Liquid Replenishment

Of most of the energy liberated during work, 75% or more is converted to heat. Body tissues can store a minor portion, less than 10% of the heat produced during prolonged, heavy muscular work; the remaining heat must be given off.

This heat loss occurs through (1) radiation to colder surroundings, (2) convection to surrounding air, (3) conduction through direct contact with colder material, and (4) moisture evaporation. Heat loss through radiation, conduction, and convection increases as weather conditions become colder and windier. Large amounts of heat can be lost through evaporation. It takes 580 kilocalories to evaporate one liter of water from the surface of the body. This heat comes from the body's heat content and therefore cools.

Photo 5
Feeding liquids during a race.

Even in ambient temperatures of −15°C, heat loss through convection and radiation is inadequate to expel the heat produced by a skier skiing at racing speed; hence, some heat must be given off by moisture evaporation, or sweating. The evaporated water comes from the body's various liquid supplies which eventually leads to liquid deficiencies in some body tissues (dehydration). Cold air is dry air and therefore considerable liquid is lost in exhaled air.

When dehydration exceeds 1-2% of body weight, performance capability is reduced even though maximum oxygen uptake and heart minute volume can be unaffected *(Fig. 21)*.

In *Table 7* are shown the results from a study where subjects worked maximally (1) after having been dehydrated by heavy muscular work for two hours, (2) after having been dehydrated by

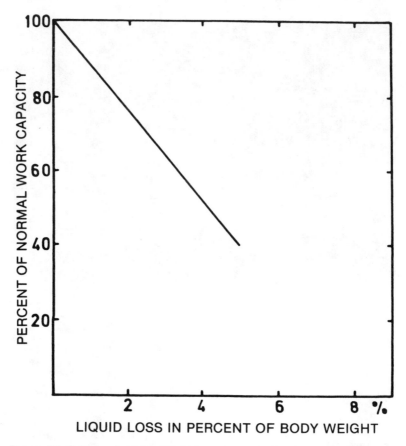

Figure 21. Relation between liquid loss and reduction of work capability. Note that a liquid loss corresponding to 2% of body weight results in a decrease in work capability to 80% of the normal. (After Saltin.)

Table 7. Maximal work at a given speed with normal liquid balance and two degrees of dehydration.

| Work | Prior to work | | Max. work |
	Liquid supply kg	Dehydration kg	Maximum duration
2 hours at 65% of maximum oxygen uptake	0	2.8	3.20
2 hours at 65% of maximum oxygen uptake	2.0	0.9	4.50
Warmup 5-10 min	0	0	5.55

heavy muscular work for two hours but with a liquid replenishment of 1 liter/hour, which reduced the degree of dehydration, and (3) with a normal liquid balance. As expected, the work capability decreased as liquid loss increased. If work capability is to be retained, liquids must be supplied such that dehydration does not exceed 1-2% of body weight.

For ski racing at temperatures of $-5°C$, liquid loss is approximately 0.5-1.2 liters/hour. For a 70 kg racer in a 30 km race (about 90 minutes racing time), this is equivalent to 1-2.2% of body weight. Liquid loss may be even greater under milder weather conditions. In training, when racers are often more heavily clothed, dehydration can be as much as 2-2.5 liter/hour.

As mentioned previously, sugar should be consumed during prolonged heavy muscular work. Therefore, it is practical to combine sugar and liquid replenishment. However, the procedure is more complex than it seems and is not yet satisfactorily solved, as sugar solutions of varying concentration leave the stomach with different speeds.

A study was made in which subjects drank sugar solutions of 5%, 10%, 20%, 30%, and 40%, as well as pure water. After one hour, the reamining liquid was pumped out of the stomach. Therefore, the amount of liquid leaving the stomach into the intestines could be calculated. The results are given in *Table 8*. The greater the sugar concentration, the less liquid exits to the intestines. Also, the liquid pumped out had higher sugar concentration.

Newer studies have addressed themselves to answering the following questions: How is the stomach's emptying speed affected by:

- Sugar concentration in the liquid (compare with the case above);
- liquid temperature and volume;
- work intensity and duration.

The following conclusions are drawn: The emptying speed of the stomach increases linearly with the consumed liquid volume up to 600 ml/15 min. A further increase of consumption did not increase emptying speed. Therefore, it is meaningless to consume more than 2.4 liters/hour, which is also an unrealistic quantity during a race *(Fig. 22)*.

The temperature of the liquid consumed apparently does not affect the stomach emptying speed very much, which is not unexpected as temperature measurements showed that liquid in the stomach assumes body temperature after one to three minutes.

In this study, subjects drank glycogen solutions with concentrations of 2.5%, 5%, 10%, and 15%. The volume remaining in the stomach was measured after 5, 10, 15, and 20 minutes. As shown in *Fig. 23,* the emptying speed decreases with increasing glucose concentration, primarily because emptying starts later with higher consumed sugar concentrations. For the 2.5% solution, the stomach is

Table 8. Volume and sugar concentration of emptied stomach liquid one hour after drinking water and solutions of varying glucose concentrations.

Glycose conc. %	0	5	10	20	40
Emptied volume ml/tim	1000	800	600	350	200
Emptied quantity sugar gram	0	40	60	70	80

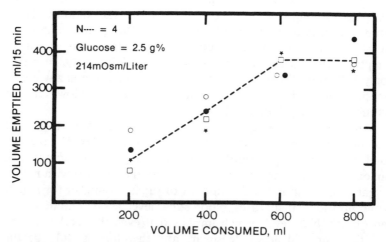

Figure 22. Stomach emptying speed as a function of consumption of liquid. (After Soderberg and Jansson.)

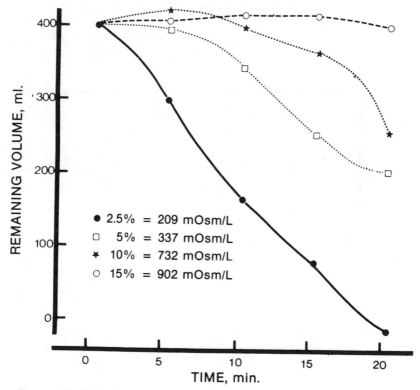

Figure 23. Stomach emptying speed when various concentrations of glucose solution are consumed. (After Soderberg and Jansson.)

completely empty after 20 minutes. The 10% solution requires 60 minutes for emptying and the 15% solution, 120 minutes. These studies were done with the subjects at rest. During work, at an intensity over 60% of maximum oxygen uptake, the stomach-emptying speed decreased with increasing work intensity, such that only 25% of the liquid consumed exits to the intestines at a work intensity of 90% of maximum oxygen uptake *(Fig. 24)*. However, this is subject to large individual variation.

When training skiing, male elite racers were "fed" a glucose solution on three consecutive days, 2.5% the first day, 5% the second day, and 18% the third; the results are given in *Table 9*. The amount of liquid emptied from the stomach decreased with higher sugar concentration but the amount of sugar was higher for higher concentrations. In all cases, blood sugar level was maintained at an adequately high level, which implies that even the weakest sugar solution supplied adequate sugar, and therefore, should be the most suitable as it provided the body with the greatest amount of liquid. However, these trials were performed during training when it is easier to consume greater quantities of liquids than in a competitive situation, when it is difficult to consume more than 1-1.5 dl at one time. As feeding every 20 minutes is suitable in racing, the amount of liquid consumed is 300-450 ml/hour. The sugar consumed is then: 2.5% solution gives 8-12 g/hour, 5% solution gives

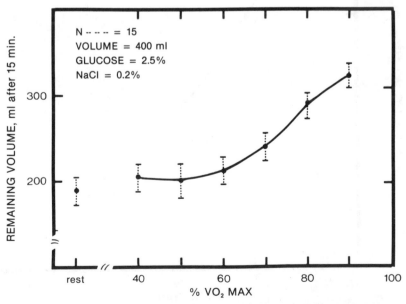

Figure 24. Liquid volume remaining in stomach at various work intensities. (After Soderberg and Jansson.)

Table 9. Consumed liquid, liquid loss, stomach emptying of sugar and liquid for different sugar solution concentrations consumed (after Soderberg and Jansson).

	Day I	Day II	Day III
Glycose concentration (%)	2.5	5	18
Consumed volume (ml)	1133	1133	600
Remaining volume	20	216	65
Quantity emptied sugar (g)	28.3	46.7	121
Worktime (min)	103	97	157
Liquid loss liter	2.7	2.3	2.3
liter/hour	1.9	1.8	1.0

15-23 g/hour, and 10% solution gives 30-45 g/hour. Because the stomach's emptying speed during heavy work varies widely with different individuals, it is not possible to exactly specify the most suitable concentration. For some individuals, the emptying speed of the stomach can be reduced to 25% of the speed for a resting situation. Then, when a 2.5% sugar solution is consumed, less than 3 g of sugar reach the intestine, which is hardly sufficient to maintain adequate blood sugar level. But, as described above, consuming a 2.5% sugar solution, especially during training, is for some individuals sufficient to maintain normal blood sugar level.

Studies have shown that an increase of blood sugar to double its normal value results in muscle glycogen during heavy work decreasing more slowly than for normal blood sugar level. Clearly, the consumed sugar is important, not just for the blood sugar level, but also for retarding the decrease of muscle glycogen, which implies that sometimes high sugar concentrations may be best.

Choice of sugar solution concentration depends on whether the primary requirement is to supply sugar, such as for racing in extreme cold or over long distances or to supply liquid, such as for summer dry-land training, ski racing at temperatures well above freezing, etc. Experience dictates that a full stomach and heavy work cannot be combined; stronger sugar solution concentrations, which leave the stomach slowly, are felt to cause nausea and feelings of weakness when consumed during training or racing. However, it is not certain whether or not stomach liquid content, with consumption of 2.5% or 15% sugar solution, sets any decisive limit to the risk of nausea and weakness. This is perhaps especially true of skiing, where body movements are less jarring than for running, which means that the stomach is not subjected to as much shock and vibration. Different individuals also react differently to the same consumed liquid, both concerning the stomach-emptying speed and reactions to large liquid quantities consumed. Therefore, each and every racer should, in training, find the type of liquid that suits him/her best for all situations. However, it may be difficult to determine the most suitable solution during a training workout, unless it stimulates competition.

In the 1950s, the Swedish elite racers did as they wished and chose a feeding station liquid comprising 3-400 grams of grape sugar per liter of water flavored with lemon, a blend having a concentration of 30-40%. This formula was used during many Winter Olympics and World Ski Championships, and with few exceptions, the racers approved of the drink. This is surprising, in light of subsequent research. For 50 km races, feeding stations were placed every 5-6 km and racers could not pass stations without drinking. It is important that feeding stations not be located too close to a steep uphill, either before or after. If possible, the ideal drinking sequence is sugar solution followed by water.

Practical Advice

Summer Training:
    Try to drink every 15-25 minutes. The warmer the weather, the more often one should drink. Drink 1-2 dl each time of 2.5-5% sugar solution.
Winter Training:
    Drink every 20 to 30 minutes of a liquid of 2.5-15% concentration at 23°-30°C.
Racing:
    If desired, 2-5 dl liquid, sugar water, or similar drink can be drunk during warmup. During a race, one should drink every 20 minutes after the first 5 km. Sugar concentration should be 2.5-15% or as dictated by experience. For extreme cold conditions,

sugar concentration can be higher than for temperatures around 0°C or warmer. Usually, it is not necessary to drink during 5 km or 10 km races or during 15 km races, unless the temperature is 0°C or above, in which case it is advantageous to drink once between 7 and 10 km.

Warning

Do not drink or eat anything resulting in a large amount of sugar in the body two to three hours before the start of a race. This can result in a body reaction (insulin secretion) that will deplete blood sugar level below the normal. Usually, such depletion is a minimum of two to three hours after sugar is consumed.

Drink Recipes:

2.5% solution

2 g table salt

25 g sugar

1 lit water

Mix well in a container. Add lemon or orange flavor or concentrate for taste.

10% solution

2 g table salt

100 g sugar

1 lit water

Mix as above. Many racers prefer grape sugar, which tastes less sweet than ordinary sugar. As for efficiency, the difference between the two sugars is negligible. Small amounts of table salts promote stomach emptying.

Ski Technique

The most customary method to assess technique is to determine oxygen uptake per kilogram body weight per minute for a given speed. The lower the oxygen uptake, the better the technique.

In running, the technique of elite runners is relatively equal but better than that for individuals who are poorer runners. This relationship most likely also applies to skiing although the differences in technique, partially among the elite racers and partially between the elite racers as a group and less skilled racers as a group, are greater than those for running. In a study of Swedish elite skiers (1960), the oxygen uptake, correspnding to covering a 10 km course in 35 minutes, was 58–62 ml/kg × min. The total spread of values was approximately 7% and applied to skiing on a horizontal track. Differences on other terrains are not stated.

Skiing, as a form of body work, differs from running in that the total rise of the body's center of gravity (on a flat track) is not as great as in running. This should imply that weight increases do not

Thomas Wassberg in the 1980 Olympic 15 km. Galen Rowell photo.

effect the same increases in energy required as they do in running. This is shown by a study in which racers ran loaded with weights in a vest. Oxygen uptake (ml/kg body weight × min) increased for a given speed *(Fig. 25a)*. But when oxygen uptake is expressed in ml/kg total weight (body weight plus weight vest) × min, it is constant, unaffected by the weight increase *(Fig. 25b)*.

This relationship is valid even for skiing uphill, but oxygen uptake per kilogram total weight decreases with increasing weight for skiing on the flat. In other words, energy requirements do not increase proportionately to body weight increases, which means that oxygen uptake per kilogram total weight decreases, even if very little. However, the subjects used skis with the same stiffness, regardless of weight increase, which probably increased friction and energy consumption. Hence, if ski stiffness had been matched to the increased weight, there would have been a greater decrease in the oxygen uptake per kilogram total weight. This means that large racers are not so disadvantaged by their size in skiing as they are in running and that an elite racer should have high oxygen uptake, both in ml/kg × min and 1/min. Persons with extremely high total oxygen uptake (1/min) should perform especially well on level tracks (on uphills the energy expense per kilogram is independent of total body weight). Among the world's elite skiers, there are examples of racers whose maximum total oxygen uptake is extremely high, but expressed in terms of body weight is 10-15% lower than the highest measured. A high body weight also results in a higher

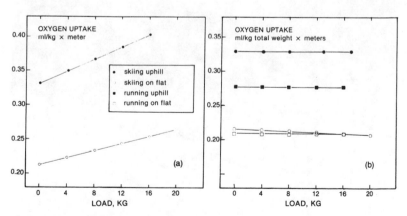

Figure 25 (a). Oxygen uptake in ml/kg × meter for increasing loads for skiing uphill and on the flat.

Figure 25 (b). Oxygen uptake in ml/kg total weight × meter for weight increase for skiing and running uphill and on the flat. (After Stattin and Lindahl.)

downhill speed. This can explain why many smaller racers, in spite of extremely high aerobic power per kilogram body weight, sometimes have difficulty competing against a larger fellow racer.

It is also highly likely that technique can diminish from one day to the next, which degrades performance capability. Experience also shows that extremely skilled racers sometimes race poorly, even though the usual factors, such as waxing or illness, are not the cause. The explanation is most likely a decrease in nervomuscular functions (see page 16).

Bill Koch in the 1976 Olympic 30 km, in which he won the silver medal. Michael Brady photo.

TRAINING

Introduction

Even though the physiological factors which differentiate elite from other racers are well known, little is known about how these differences are produced. In other words, knowledge is lacking on the factors which stimulate development, for instance, of high maximum oxygen-uptake capability. Therefore, it is impossible to exactly outline the most effective training for any athletic event. The principles most used thus far to delineate training programs are to simulate competitive conditions as closely as possible and to copy the training practiced by the world champions in the athletic event in question (especially if his/her training program comprises unique activities). However, the latter method is not necessarily recommended, as a top athlete may well become world champion in spite of the unique training forms practiced.

The contribution of physiology to training has first and foremost been to understand how, for instance, respiration and circulation improve during various types of maximum work, to understand various physiological variables (pulse, oxygen uptake, blood lactic acid level) in the competitive situation, and under the assumption that training should simulate competition as much as possible, formulate guidelines for training.

Oxygen Transport Training

Elite racers are known to have very high oxygen-uptake capability and that their oxygen-transport organs are loaded maximally or almost maximally in racing. Therefore, a major portion of training should aim to improve the functioning of these oxygen-transport organs. This can be achieved by:

- increasing the maximum oxygen transport;
- the capability to exploit these increases as much as possible over longer periods of time.

The basic principle for increasing maximum oxygen uptake is to load the oxygen-transport system maximally or almost maximally, which is why training tempo should be high. However, this soon results in lactic acid concentration in the muscles such that subsequently (after 10-20 min) tempo must be reduced, which reduces the load on the heart and lungs. To counteract this effect and to hold oxygen uptake at or near maximum for most of a long workout, it is necessary to alternate between hard and easy tempo (or rest). This is accomplished by various forms of interval training.

Long Intervals

Activity periods of 2-10 minutes, interspersed with 2-5 minute periods of lesser activity or rest. Repeated 3-10 times. Most easily performed if activity periods are 3-7 minutes long. At the end of each activity period, the heart rate should be no more than 10 below its maximum rate *(Fig. 26)*.

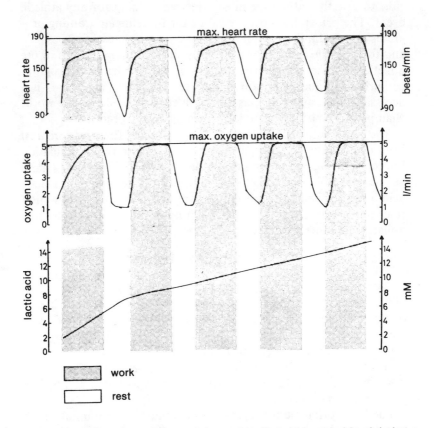

Figure 26. Heart rate, oxygen uptake, and lactic acid level in blood during an interval training program with four-minute activity periods and two-minute rests. (After Karlsson et al.)

Short Intervals

Activity periods of 60-90 seconds, interspersed with 20-30 second periods of lesser activity or rest. Because activity periods are less than two minutes long, it is not possible to accelerate oxygen uptake from rest level up to maximum. Therefore, rests should be shortened so that oxygen uptake does not sink excessively before the next activity period starts *(Fig. 27)*. Heart rate should be no more than 10 below its maximum rate at the end of each activity period.

Short-Short Intervals

Activity periods of 10-20 seconds, interspersed with 5-15 second periods of lesser activity or rest, continued for a total of 20-60 minutes. Tempo should be higher than for long or short interval training, which apparently would result in high lactic acid buildup. However, studies have shown that short-short interval training can be conducted without undue increase of muscular or blood lactic acid level.

This may be ascribed to myoglobin being "charged up" with oxygen during the rest periods. This oxygen can then prevent large oxygen debt during the activity periods. Example: Interval training with 15-second activity periods and 10-second rest periods, at a tempo requiring an oxygen uptake of 7.5-1/min, corresponds to

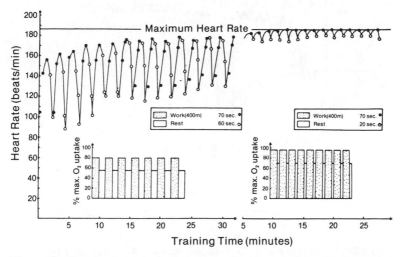

Figure 27. Heart rate and oxygen uptake (in percent of maximum oxygen uptake) during running unprepared 70-second activity periods interspersed respectively with 60- and 20-second rest periods. (After Karlsson et al.)

1.75 liter per activity period. If the individual involved has a capacity to take up 1.25 liter oxygen per activity period, an oxygen debt of 0.5 liter is incurred. During the rest period the oxygen uptake is 0.6 liter. Because the body's oxygen needs during rest are approximately 0.3 lit/min = 0.05 liter per rest period, each rest period results in a surplus of 0.55 liter, which can go to "charge up" the myoglobin. If the activity periods are prolonged to 30 seconds, the oxygen stored in the myoglobin is insufficient and energy must be transferred anaerobically (via glycolysis) with the resultant buildup of lactic acid.

It may be difficult to make progress with this type of training as it requires exact balance between activity periods, rest periods, and tempo *(Fig. 28)*.

Natural Interval

Natural interval training involves running or skiing in varying terrain for 45-120 minutes. This type of training is a mixture of all the types of interval training mentioned above. On uphills, oxygen uptake is maximum or nearly maximum, while it is considerably less on downhills *(Fig. 29)*. At the ends of the uphills, pulse should be 10-15 beats/minute under the maximum pulse rate.

This is the most used form of training among ski racers (who often call it distance training).

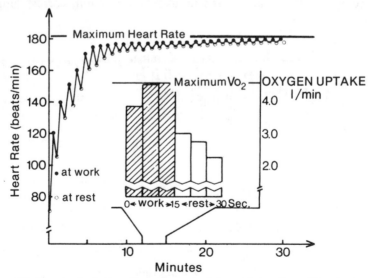

Figure 28. Heart rate during 15 × 15 sec training, a form of condition training with short activity and rest periods (15 sec). Oxygen uptake for this type of training is maximum, but blood lactic acid can be held low if the correct intensity during activity periods is maintained. (After Christenssen et al.)

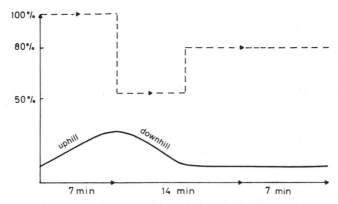

Figure 29. Oxygen uptake requirements in percent of maximum oxygen uptake capability for Assar Ronnlund and Karl-Ake Asph, distance running in varied terrain. Solid line is terrain profile, dotted line is oxygen uptake. (After Karlsson et al.)

Tempo Training

Tempo training involves skiing at racing speed for 10-25 minutes, interspersed with slower skiing, and resembles natural interval training. However, in tempo training, speed is higher, primarily on uphills which results in a higher blood lactate acid level. Tempo training is used, of course, immediately before and during the racing season.

Suitable Tempo For Interval Training
(Long And Short Intervals)

Assume that an athlete can run 1500 meters in 4 minutes, 30 seconds, which corresponds to an average speed of 20 km/h. If this is the maximum performance for the athlete, then energy must be delivered both aerobically and anaerobically with considerable lactic acid buildup as a result. As interval training mostly aims to load the oxygen-transport system, it is unnecessary to select a training tempo that requires a large anaerobic contribution. A suitable speed is then that which maximally loads the oxygen-transport system. In this case, the speed should be 17-18 km/h which corresponds to 5 min, 20 sec for 1500 meters. A suitable speed for the individual in Fig. 14, No. 2 is then 22 km/h. Running "hard" can result in paying the price for excess tempo: high lactic acid buildup.

Distance Training

Distance training (sometimes called "quantity" training) usually describes training at an even tempo over longer time periods, one to four hours or more. During distance training, heart rate and oxygen uptake are clearly under their maximum levels, and as a consequence, it is hardly the best training for increasing maximum oxygen uptake.

Distance training aims primarily to enhance the capability for exploiting a large portion of aerobic power over longer time periods. A comparison of Swedish elite racers and well-trained GIH physical education students during a 90-minute distance workout showed that the elite skiers exploited higher percentages of their maximum oxygen uptake while, in most cases, having a lower blood lactic acid level. This was the case both for running and for roller skiing (*Fig. 30*, Table 11). Whether this is due to the elite skiers having trained longer distances or due to genetic inheritance cannot be determined now. (An interesting observation is that the elite skier subjects had 72-91% slow muscle fibers in their leg muscles compared to 63-64% for the GIH physical education students.)

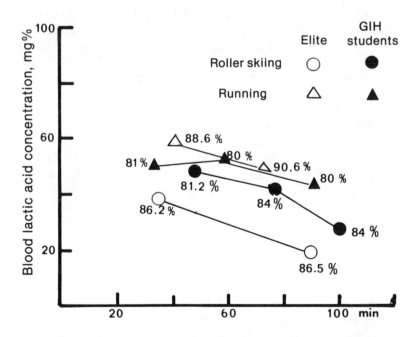

Figure 30. Blood lactic acid concentration during distance training in the form of roller skiing and running. During roller skiing, the elite skiers' blood lactic acid level was lower than that of the GIH physical education students, although they loaded their oxygen-transport systems more. For running, concentrations were equal, despite the skiers' relative oxygen uptake being 90% compared to the students' 80%.

Experience dictates that it is necessary for elite skiers to train a few times a week over distances in excess of their racing distances. Perhaps this training is necessary to effect certain local changes in muscles? See page 35. There are also many examples of racers who have improved from year to year, despite their oxygen uptake remaining unaltered. Part of such improvement can be ascribed to improved technique, but part is most likely due to improved muscle fiber function. As discussed previously, training also promotes the muscles' capability to burn fatty acids, which saves glycogen. Training is often increased by increasing the duration of each workout.

Effect Of Different Forms Of Oxygen-Transport Training

Studies of Swedish Army recruits showed that the effects of distance training (30 min), long interval training (3 min activity, 3 min rest), and short-short interval (15 sec activity, 15 sec rest, for a duration of 30 min) by in large resulted in the same increase (20%) in maximum oxygen uptake over a period of two months. Hence, one may conclude that these forms of training are essentially equally effective. However, one should consider that the group in question comprised relatively untrained persons. Thus far, it is not possible to say which form of training is best for elite ski racers. This is why today's elite skiers, who spend a considerable amount of time training, use various forms of training. Most used are distance training and natural interval training, as well as some long intervals in the form of running, roller skiing, or skiing gradual uphills (5-15 min). How much is interval and how much is distance training is often a question of definition. That is, training which some may call distance training, is called natural interval by others (see further, page 62). Because characteristics vary considerably from individual to individual (size of heart, muscle mass, combination of muscle fibers, etc.), it is obvious that the ideal training program must be tailor-made for *one* person, not for a whole group.

Studies Of Elite Training

Dry-land training

Skiers dry-land train by running and roller skiing, often with running being dominant. The total number of workouts and training hours for elite skiers as well as division between roller skiing and running are given in *Table 10*.

Running - The typical behavior of heart frequency during a

Table 10. Roller skiing training in percent of total training hours and workouts (totals in parentheses).

Category		% training hours		% of workouts	
Nat. train.	Men	46	(5.0)	45	(2.7)
Group 1	Men	14	(0.9)	17	(1.0)
Test Group	Men	19	(1.4)	16	(1.0)
Average	Men	26	(2.4)	26	(1.6)
Nat. train.	Women	47	(3.7)	36	(2.3)
Group 1	Women	42	(2.8)	34	(2.5)
Test Group	Women	35	(2.3)	26	(2.0)
Average	Women	41	(2.9)	32	(2.3)
High school	Men	41	(3.0)	30	(2.5)
students	Women	39	(2.5)	27	(2.0)
Average		35		29	

Bild 6
Syreupptagningsbestämning vid rullskidåkning.

Photo 6
Measuring oxygen uptake during roller skiing.

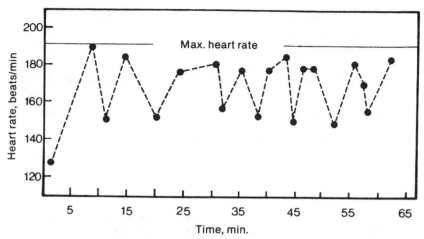

Figure 31. Heart frequency during a 60-minute workout. For the subject, a heart frequency of 180 beats/minute corresponds to 90-95% of maximum oxygen uptake. The points are measured data frequencies. The behavior of the frequency between data points is not known, so the points are connected with dashed lines.

60-minute workout with constant running is shown in *Fig. 31*. It is obvious that this is a case of natural interval training.

Heart frequency behavior for another racer on a 90-minute training workout is shown in *Fig. 32*. This is called distance training,

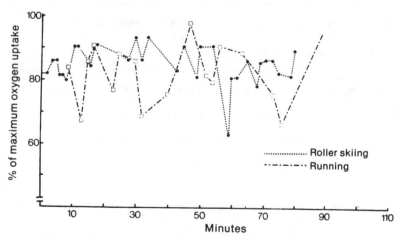

Figure 32. Oxygen uptake during roller skiing and running in hilly terrain. The elevation difference between the highest and lowest points on the running course was about 55 meters, while the corresponding difference for the roller ski course was 145 meters. However, the total elevation gain (and loss) around the two courses was approximately the same.

Table 11. Oxygen uptake, heart rate, blood lactic acid level during maximum work, and distance training by roller skiing and running. Figures in parentheses are oxygen uptake in percent of the highest measured for the subjects involved. *Average oxygen uptake in percent of maximum during five minutes immediately preceding test.

Maximum work (5-7 min)

Running			Rollerskiing		
Oxygen uptake 1/min	Heart rate beats/min	Lactate mg %	Oxygen uptake 1/min	Heart rate beats/min	Lactate mg %
A 5.05	189	118	4.96 (98)	186	94
B 3.74	188	126	3.60 (96)	182	92
C -	-	-	-	-	-

Distance training (85-110 min)

Running			Rollerskiing		
Oxygen uptake 1/min	Heart rate beats/min	Lactate mg %	Oxygen uptake 1/min	Heart rate beats/min	Lactate mg %
A 4.13 (79)	178	50 (80)*	4.29 (82)	178	39 (80)
B -	-	-	-	-	-
C 4.71 (83)	148	56 (90)*	4.84 (85)	158	29 (87)

A	GIH - Stud	n = 2
B	Female elite	n = 4
C	Male elite	n = 4

which could be questioned as the data may indicate natural interval.

Roller skiing - Skiers most often roller ski for 20 to 40 km continuously. The dominant stride is double poling with a single kick;

the diagonal stride is used only on the steeper uphills. In most cases, oxygen uptake is about 85% of the maximum (as measured during running). On steep uphills it may be almost maximum (Fig. 32 and 36).

Ski Striding - Norwegian studies by Hermansen have shown that dry-land ski striding with poles on steeper uphills can load the oxygen-transport system maximally. This type of training is used mostly in irregular, steep terrain, where ordinary running results in local fatigue in leg muscles. Arm and shoulder muscles are, of course, trained at the same time.

Comparison Of Roller Skiing To Running

The oxygen uptake for maximum roller skiing is essentially the same as that for maximum running uphill (*Table 11* and *Fig. 33*).

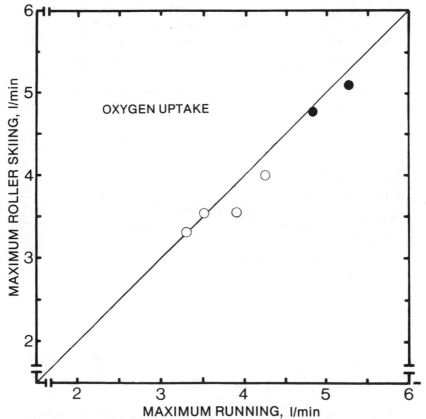

Figure 33. Oxygen uptake during maximum roller skiing and maximum running (4-7 min roller skiing, respectively running uphill) **o** = female elite skiers, **•** = GIH students.

For a one to two hour workout, roller skiing can load the oxygen-transport system just as much, or more than running (Table 11 and Fig. 32). Therefore, it is reasonable to assume that roller skiing and running are equal forms of training oxygen transport. In addition, roller skiing is excellent strength training for arm and trunk muscles. However, roller skiing probably does not train leg muscles as does running, as roads, where roller skis are used, seldom have as steep uphills as do the trails where racers customarily run.

It is unlikely that roller skiing is useful for technique training, quite the contrary: Most likely it imbues unwanted movements. For experienced racers who master ski technique well there is little risk that roller skiing can degrade on-ski technique. However, one cannot exclude the possibility that very young racers who roller ski extensively adopt a movement pattern which can complicate the learning of good ski technique.

Roller skiing also provides variation in off-snow, dry-land training, which is why it is often possible to train more than by just running. Often, when injuries prevent running, it is still possible to roller ski. However, there are cases when excessive roller skiing has led to overuse injuries, primarily on the front of the shin.

Ski Training - Ski training has not been systematically investigated in this study. However, a couple of studies have been made of on-ski training workouts. One study *(Fig. 34)* was done in the end of

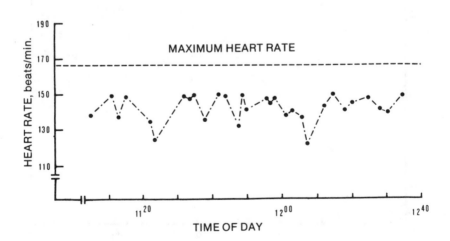

Figure 34. Heart rate during the second and third hours of a four–hour-long workout on skis. The median heart rate corresponds to an oxygen uptake of 80% maximum. However, when the skier stopped to drink the heart rate dropped below 130 beats/min.

November, the transition to snow period. The workout was four hours long. The average oxygen uptake was approximately 80% of maximum. The other study *(Fig. 35)* was conducted in mid January during a 90-minute-long workout. Most of the time, the heart rate was 10-20 beats/minute under maximum, which implies a high load on the oxygen-transport system.

Measurements made during training the week prior to important races show that racers' heart rates on uphills are mostly 5-10 beats/min below maximum.

Strength Training

Even though oxygen-transport training dominates for cross–country ski racers, strength training is extremely important.

The results of many studies show that the effect of strength training is on the muscle groups and the type of strength trained. That is, the training of dynamic endurance increases this type of strength considerably but has little effect on other types of strength. In addition, dynamic endurance training may mean that a movement is performed with, for instance, 30% of maximum strength for one minute or with 10% of maximum strength for 30 minutes. Here, the effect of training is greatest at the load used and considerably less for other loads.

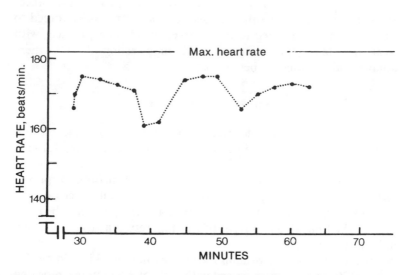

Figure 35. Heart rate during portions of a 90-minute workout on skis. For this racer 170 beats/min corresponds to 93-95% of maximum oxygen uptake.

It is also extremely important to analyze which muscles are used in skiing and how they work, statically or dynamically, maximum strength or endurance strength.

As extensive studies are not made, the situation will be analyzed here subjectively and through comparison with other similar work forms.

Skiing is primarily dynamic work, characterized by endurance for most body muscles, primarily the arm and leg muscles. However, some muscles sustain long-duration static loads, such as leg and trunk muscles, primarily on downhills. On certain parts of courses, relatively large dynamic power is needed, such as on steep uphills and when double-poling sprinting across a finish line. Therefore, during training it is best to have a few maximum sprints a week, 5-10 seconds up a steep uphill, interspersed with easy skiing 30-60 seconds, repeated 10-20 times, as well as maximum double poling for 30 seconds, interspersed with easy skiing, repeated 10-20 times. This is especially important training for relay racing.

In dry-land training, strength training can be performed as roller skiing, ski striding uphill, or with arm exercisers, such as elastic cords, primarily with light loads. Weight training with heavier weights has often been in vogue with ski racers. In running or skiing, one seldom uses more than 10-20% of maximum strength in any maneuver; training with heavy weights is, at least theoretically, unnecessary. It will soon be a thing of the past.

Strength is also decisive for ski technique, because all maneuvers require certain strengths for correct, prolonged performance. When a particular strength is inadequate, a racer may be forced to use a maneuver unsuited to the course; for instance, a racer with weak arms may ski the diagonal stride on a section of track where double-poling would be better.

Anaerobic Training

The effects of anaerobic training are not yet fully understood. However, anaerobic training is a necessary part of training for elite skiers, especially for those who race 5 km, 10 km, and relays.

Anaerobic training aims to promote muscle function, in spite of large lactic acid buildup. Therefore, training should focus on the same muscles as are used in competition and tempo should be maximum. The following two types of training result in large lactic acid buildup in muscles:

● maximum skiing, running, roller skiing or ski striding for 60-120 seconds, interspersed with rests of 4-8 minutes, repeated 5-10 times. The rest periods should comprise light activity, not complete rest.

● as above with activity periods of 30-60 seconds, interspersed with 60-90 second rests, repeated 5-10 times.

At the end of each sprint the muscles used should feel "dead tired"; one should feel unable to take another step. This type of training is extremely taxing and therefore should not be done in the last one or two months prior to important races.

The tactical preparation for racing should include training at racing tempo. This is how a racer learns how much anaerobic work he/she tolerates without degrading overall capability. As discussed previously, this is especially important for racing at higher altitudes. Relay starts are tricky and the anaerobic processes are certainly a contributing factor. It is easy to start with a tempo so high that excess lactic acid builds up.

Technique Training

Technique training aims to improve technique and hence the training activity should use the movements to be improved. For skiers, this means that skiing is the best form of technique training.

In the beginning, technique should be trained in easy terrain at a relatively low tempo, sometimes, if needed, without poles to improve balance and rhythm. Subsequently, as technique improves, training should be on more demanding tracks at higher tempo.

For younger skiers, technique training is especially important in the growth years. This is when good coaches should direct training so that poor technique does not become habit. Thereafter it is wise not to experiment too much with one's skiing style.

Subsequent skiing in all types of terrain and snow conditions helps polish technique.

As a rule, technique training should focus on a skier's poorest maneuvers, as this is where the greatest improvement can be made.

It is well known that technique can be constant for many years while muscular strength and condition can vary from week to week. Hence, there is little need to practice technique per se on the first on-ski training tours of a winter season. In the change over to skiing period there is little need to polish technique but rather a need for the body to become accustomed to the "new" activity.

Quantity Of Training And Amount Of Training Of Different Forms

These data are based on analyses conducted in 1973 by Jan Hallin. It should be stressed that training quantity and intensity have varied through the years, subject to current fad, so it is often difficult to determine what is vital and what is unimportant in any one racer's training program.

R. Smetanina in the 1980 Olympic 5 km, which she won. Galen Rowell photo.

Amount Of Roller Skiing

Most senior racers spend 40-45% of their total dry-land training time on roller skis but devote a lower percentage of their total number of workouts to roller skiing (Table 10). Roller ski workouts are longer, which may be because blood lactic acid buildup is lower in roller skiing despite the oxygen uptake being about the same as for running. Some racers probably can load their oxygen-transport systems more when roller skiing than when running.

Amount Of Training

Most male elite racers train every day and on the average two hours per workout. Female elite racers often train as often as men but their average time per workout is less *(Table 12)*. This is logical as women's race distances are shorter than those for men. Some racers train more than these averages.

Amounts Of Distance And Interval Training

Distance training dominates year-round although mostly towards the end of dry-land training *(Table 13)*. Here, natural interval training is classified as distance training. Because skiers train mostly in rolling terrain, their training usually has an interval character. If this type of training is then classified as interval training, the result certainly will be that interval training is dominant for most of the year, except for the first training period on skis.

The question is whether distance training as it is defined on page 58 is practiced to any great extent, except during the initial period on skis.

To a great extent, terrain determines the effect of training (compare *Figs. 32 & 37)*. Training with fairly constant tempo in relatively level terrain results in a more constant work load than training in more hilly terrain where work load is greater on uphills and lesser on downhills.

Racing Tactics

Racers should ski a course at least twice before a race so that they know the locations of all difficult and easy parts.

In individual events the object is to cover a given distance in as little time as possible. This is easiest when *tempo is held as constant as possible* (load on the oxygen-transport system as constant as possible).

Table 12. Total training hours and total number of workouts prior to and during the racing season. Figures in parentheses are highest and lowest values. Times shown are effective training times and do not include transportation, warmup, etc.

	Autumn		Racing season	
	Workouts/week	Hours/week	Workouts/week	Hours/week
Men Elite	7.7 (10.3-7.3)	15.7 (18.2-10.0)	4.7 (5.5-4.3)	6.4 (7.1-4.1)
Women Elite	7.7 (8.4-7.3)	12.2 (12.9-10.8)	5.7 (6.7-5.3)	6.8 (7.2-3.4)

Table 13. Amount of interval training and comparison of interval and distance training.

Dry land v41-44 1972	Initial skiing v45-49 1972	Racing season v49/1972-v13/1973
34%	1.8%	15%

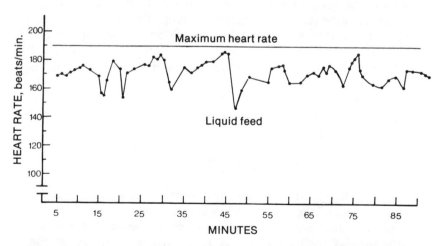

Figure 36. Heart rate during a 90-minute roller ski tour on a hilly road. Rate of 180 beats/min corresponds, for the subject, to 90-93% of maximum oxygen uptake.

The situation differs for a mass start. Of course, the racer capable of maintaining the highest average speed will beat the competition but occasionally results are decided in sprints at the finish.

The tactics for individual starts should be to ski at as steady a pace as possible, which means that one should not ski as fast as possible up hills with no margin left. Time gained in skiing a few uphills as fast as possible may be lost when speed drops on subsequent parts of the course. Racers who are "finished" lose time even on downhills. Constant pace is especially important when courses go above 1000 meters elevation above sea level.

When you try to sprint away from or "shake off" a competitor, you should:

- start a sprint on that part of the course you ski best and/or your competitor skis poorest, and
- try to gain a good lead before the next downhill so your competitor cannot ski behind you, using you to break wind to his/her advantage.

If you race neck and neck with a competitor, it is best to try to sprint away from him/her directly; otherwise you may fall into his/her tempo.

If a competitor passes you but does not ski faster then you should try to "hang on," as it is easier to ski just behind someone than to be in the lead.

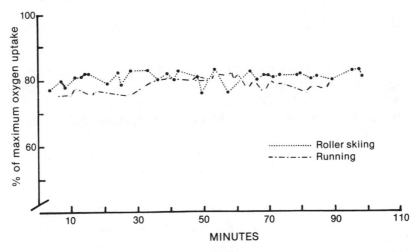

Figure 37. Oxygen uptake for roller skiing and running in slightly hilly terrain. Work load on the oxygen-transport system is fairly constant throughout the workout. Terrain character can be very important in determining the effect of training. Training in hilly terrain has more of an interval character than training in relatively flat terrain. (Compare to Fig. 32 & Fig. 36)

If the first few kilometers of the course have long or steep uphills, you should warm up more than usual, that is, with a higher tempo (see page 28).

Illness/Injury—Training And Racing

Injuries in dry-land training are not infrequent. Most common are overuse injuries of heel tendons, knee joints, and shin splints. Most of this type of injury can be avoided by sensible planning of training. If injured, training should stop to allow the injured part to rest. When the injury has healed, training should be resumed at an easy tempo to prevent the injury from reoccurring.

However cautious, most racers have at one time or another been plagued by sickness and/or injury. The question is then: What should I do about training and racing? No general answer can be given but one general rule is:

NEVER TRAIN HARD AND NEVER RACE WHEN YOU HAVE AN INFECTION OR ARE OTHERWISE IN POOR HEALTH. IF POSSIBLE, SEEK THE ADVICE OF A PHYSICIAN. DO NOT TRAIN OR COMPETE IF YOU

a) have a fever;

b) have a sore throat (red swollen, and/or with excess mucus);

c) have a bad cold;

d) have just been vaccinated (check with the doctor concerned).

YOU CAN TRAIN EASILY BUT SHOULD NOT TRAIN HARD OR COMPETE IF YOU

a) have recently been ill;

b) have a light cold (slightly blocked nose with no fever or sore throat);

c) have had, for any reason, a long break in training (applies primarily to initial period after training is resumed).

IF YOU HAVE BEEN ILL DO NOT RESUME TRAINING UNTIL **YOU ARE COMPLETELY WELL**—CONSULT YOUR PHYSICIAN.

Avoid **hard training and racing** in extremely cold weather, −15°C and colder.

If you have a cold or other contagious condition, do *not* train, race, or go to training camps with other athletes. If you are uncertain, consult your physician and/or coach.

Joan Groothuysen (Canada) in the 1980 Olympic 10 km. Barbara Brewster photo.

Clothing

Remember

- to always have enough overclothing both for training and racing;
- to always change to warm, dry clothing after activity (if possible, change to dry underwear);
- to avoid sitting in a cold vehicle or other cold places, especially after training or racing;
- that the lower abdomen and groin are particularly sensitive to cooling and that urinary problems are often long-lasting or chronic and are difficult to cure completely.

TO RACE WHEN YOU ARE NOT COMPLETELY WELL IS MISGUIDED LOYALTY TO YOUR TEAMMATES, CLUB, OR ORGANIZATION AND LEADERS. RACING WHEN YOU ARE ILL CAN HAVE SERIOUS CONSEQUENCES; IN SO DOING YOU MAY RISK YOUR HEALTH OR YOUR LIFE!

Follow Up

Learning modern training is the way to get the most out of training and racing. It is important to follow training and racing by keeping a training diary, detailed and accurate such that you can subsequently evaluate the results of training and racing. You then can evaluate:

- effect of the various methods of training;
- race results, time for peaking;
- which waxes are best on which snows;
- if there are any snow conditions and/or course profiles where you always perform poorly.

Testing

Both coaches and racers should have an objective measure of the effect of training on the cardiovascular system. For instance, a lowered pulse for a given, unchanged submaximal load on a cycle ergometer indicates that heart stroke volume has increased, evidence that training has improved oxygen transport. In such testing, it is important that the work load is constant from test to test; pulse measurement is the parameter used to assess and check condition. Computation of maximum oxygen uptake provides no further information and besides is relatively inaccurate.

Another reason to recommend regular testing is that results will show a "dip" if the subject has an infection. If a racer has been exposed to and feels that he/she is coming down with a cold or other infection, testing can often reveal whether or not heart rate is normal. In such a case, data for comparison must be available, such as from earlier tests when the athlete was completely healthy.

Also to be recommended are occasional electrocardiograms (ECG) tests both when at rest and when active in a work test. If ECG changes are noted simultaneously with a suspected infection, comparison with an earlier ECG will more readily reveal whether or not the changes can be ascribed to pathological causes.

Olympic relay race teams have been chosen on the basis of results from cycle ergometer tests. Such an approach may be valid if the choice is between several, outwardly apparently equal racers. The assumption must then be that results from previous tests as well as race results are available for all individuals tested.

Work intensity
Male seniors: 1200-1500 kpm/min = 200-250 watts.
Female seniors: 750-900 kpm/min = 125-150 watts.
Male juniors: 900-1500 kpm/min = 150-250 watts.
Female juniors: 600-900 kpm/min = 100-150 watts.
Test frequency: 8-12 times a year

General Observations

Aside from the requisite ability, being an elite skier requires so much training to exploit all possibilities for physical development that it cannot be accomplished in one or two years. One reason is that an individual needs a well-trained body to tolerate the level of training now required of elite skiers.

There is no doubt that training for oxygen transport should dominate a ski racer's training program. However, as yet nobody knows exactly which form of training is the most effective. Also, it is unlikely that any one training program would suit all persons because of individual differences such as muscle fiber composition. In today's situation it would be incorrect to categorically state that any one type of training is superior to all others for all persons.

Studies have shown that the possibility of affecting the size of bodily organs is maximum during a person's growth years. Hence, it is important that training starts relatively early at an age of 10 to 12 years. This initial training should not be too hard: Harder, more extensive training can wait. Girls generally develop earlier than boys and can start more serious training when they are about 13 years old, but boys should wait until they are about 15 years old. This applies to oxygen-transport training. Extensive strength training and anaerobic training should start a few years later.

It is important that training be regular and that it **gradually** increase both in amount and intensity.

All experience indicates that long, hard, basic physical training results in a longer and more stable form peak than does a shorter burst of training a few months a season.

Maximum oxygen transport increases most rapidly during the first few years of training and thereafter increases by lesser amounts *(Fig. 38)*. Several studies have shown that the maximum aerobic power changes little after four to six years of regular, hard training. As a consequence, the first few years of training should aim to increase maximum oxygen uptake using predominantly interval forms of training. Thereafter, training can concentrate on other forms, such as endurance training. If training is done in hilly terrain, it may be difficult to determine what is interval training and what is distance training (see page 71). If the intent is to interval train, speed should be greater up hills and lesser downhills and on the flat than if the intent is to distance train.

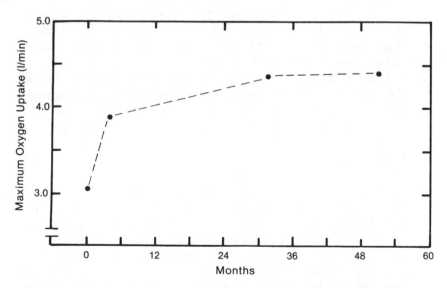

Figure 38. Effect of regular training on maximum oxygen uptake. The greatest change occurs in the first training year; thereafter increases are smaller.

Photo 7
Heart rate measured during a roller ski race. Photo and graph for the same event.